Washington

Washington

Jean F. Blashfield

Children's Press®
A Division of Grolier Publishing
New York London Hong Kong Sydney
Danbury, Connecticut

Frontispiece: Mount Baker

Front cover: The Seattle skyline at dusk

Back cover: Colorful houseboats at the Gasworks Park marina
on Lake Union

Consultant: Edward Nolan, head of Special Collections, Washington State Historical Society

Please note: All statistics are as up-to-date as possible at the time of publication.

Visit Children's Press on the Internet at http://publishing.grolier.com

Book production by Editorial Directions, Inc.

Library of Congress Cataloging-in-Publication Data

Blashfield, Jean F.
    Washington / Jean F. Blashfield.
        144 p. 24 cm. — (America the beautiful. Second series)
    Includes bibliographical references (p.) and index.
    ISBN 0-516-21095-5
    1. Washington (State)—Juvenile literature. [1. Washington (State)] I. Title. II. Series.
F891.3 .B58 2001
979.7—dc21   00-029512
                                                                        CIP
                                                                         AC

©2001 by Children's Press®, a division of Grolier Publishing Co., Inc.
All rights reserved. Published simultaneously in Canada
Printed in the United States of America
1 2 3 4 5 6 7 8 9 10 R 10 09 08 07 06 05 04 03 02 01

Acknowledgments

Like all writers, I am indebted to librarians. They are the people who treasure information, delight in organizing it, relish confirming it, and rejoice in sharing it. My special thanks for assistance in preparing this book go to the Washington State Historical Society; the Hedberg Public Library in Janesville, Wisconsin; the University of Wisconsin in Madison Memorial Library (and their fine catalog on the Internet); and the State Historical Society of Wisconsin.

Mount Rainier
National Park

The lighthouse at Lime Kiln Point

Olympic National Park

Statue of Chief Sealth

Contents

Cross-country skiing in the
Cascade Mountains

Space Needle at the heart
of Seattle's skyline

Crates of apples

Purple shore crab

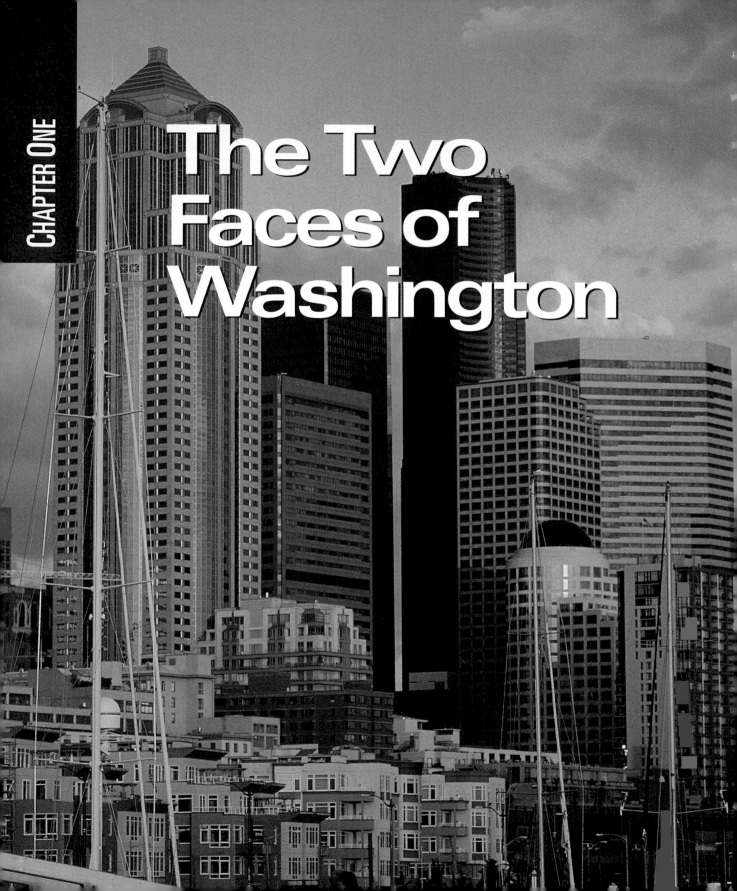

CHAPTER ONE

The Two Faces of Washington

For decades, outsiders thought of Washington as simply the most northwestern of the original forty-eight states. They thought Washington offered nothing more than one of America's highest mountains and lots and lots of evergreen trees—enough to give it the nickname of the Evergreen State.

But Washingtonians knew they had a well-kept secret. They knew their state offered an incredible variety of scenery, a comfortable climate, an energetic business life, and much more.

Washington is known as the Evergreen State because of its vast forests.

Toward the end of the twentieth century, Washington took on a new appeal. In 1994, when Jeff Bezos, a young man from Texas, was dreaming up a way to sell books on the Internet, he headed to Seattle, the biggest city in Washington. He wanted to learn all he could from the city's booksellers and various computer gurus. He and his wife started Amazon.com in a spare bedroom of their home in Bellevue, a suburb of Seattle. Their success selling books online makes them believe they can sell just about anything on the Internet.

In 1999, *Time* magazine named Jeff Bezos its Person of the Year. Reporter Joshua Cooper Ramo said of Jeff Bezos: "[His]

Opposite: The view from Seattle's Bell Harbor marina

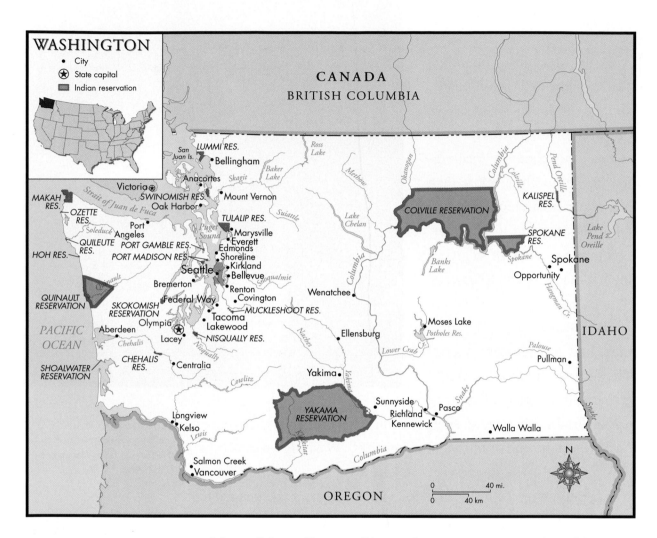

WASHINGTON
- • City
- ⭐ State capital
- ▬ Indian reservation

CANADA
BRITISH COLUMBIA

Ross Lake

Baker Lake

Skagit

Methow

Okanogan

Columbia

Colville

Pend Oreille

Lake Pend Oreille

San Juan Is.

LUMMI RES.
• Bellingham

Anacortes

Victoria ⊛

SWINOMISH RES.
Oak Harbor
• Mount Vernon

MAKAH RES.

Strait of Juan de Fuca

OZETTE RES.

Soleduck

QUILEUTE RES.

HOH RES.

Port Angeles

Puget Sound

TULALIP RES.
• Marysville
• Everett
Edmonds
Shoreline
• Kirkland

PORT GAMBLE RES.

PORT MADISON RES.

Seattle
• Bellevue

Bremerton

Renton

• Covington

Federal Way

Suiattle

Lake Chelan

KALISPEL RES.

COLVILLE RESERVATION

SPOKANE RES.

Banks Lake

Spokane

• Spokane

Opportunity

Snohomish

Snoqualmie

Wenatchee

Columbia

QUINAULT RESERVATION

Quinault

SKOKOMISH RESERVATION

MUCKLESHOOT RES.

Tacoma
Lakewood

Olympia ⭐

Lacey

Aberdeen

Chehalis

PACIFIC OCEAN

SHOALWATER RESERVATION

CHEHALIS RES.

NISQUALLY RES.

Nisqually

• Centralia

Cowlitz

Naches

Ellensburg

Moses Lake

• Potholes Res.

Lower Crab

Palouse

IDAHO

Pullman

Yakima

YAKAMA RESERVATION

Sunnyside

Richland
Kennewick

Pasco

Snake

Walla Walla

Longview

Kelso

Lewis

Klickitat

Columbia

Salmon Creek
Vancouver

OREGON

N

0   40 mi.
0   40 km

Geopolitical map of Washington

vision of the online retailing universe was so complete, his Amazon.com site so elegant and appealing, that it became from Day One the point of reference for anyone who had anything to sell online. And that, it turns out, is everyone." The confidence and creativity that made Bezos's idea flourish are what make Seattle and Washington tick.

Jeff Bezos (left) appearing on *The Tonight Show* with Jay Leno

Two Washingtons

Washington's Cascade Mountains divide the state right down the middle, from north to south. These mountains separate Washington into two different climates, economies, and histories.

But these two Washingtons do not produce two kinds of Washingtonians. The people of Washington stick together. They are all proud of their state and its creative thinkers.

Misnaming Washington

When Washington Territory was created out of Oregon Territory, many people wanted it to be called Columbia Territory, after the great Columbia River. However, federal officials were concerned that it might be mistaken for the District of Columbia. So they named it for George Washington, the first president of the United States. However, it is still mistaken for the District of Columbia, which is called Washington, D.C. ■

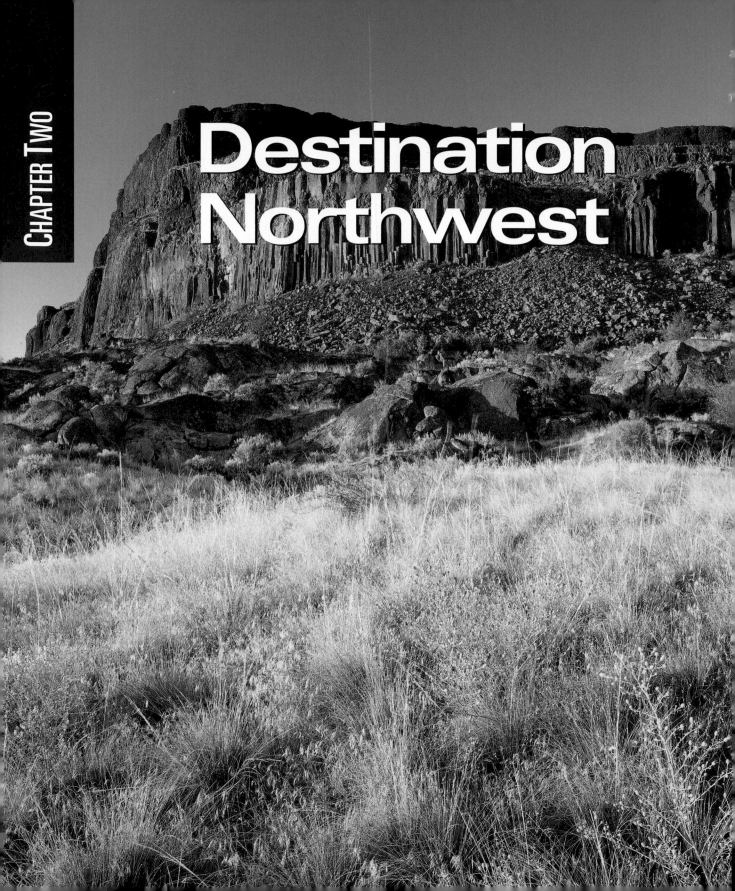

CHAPTER TWO

Destination Northwest

Scientists have found evidence that humans lived on the west coast of North America 25,000 years ago. It is likely that they also lived in—or at least passed through—the area that eventually became Washington. At that time, the huge glaciers of the ice ages covered much of the land. So much water was tied up in ice that a land bridge between Russia and Alaska may have been visible.

Native Americans catching salmon in the Columbia River

As the glaciers retreated, these early Native Americans lived by fishing and by hunting large mammals such as woolly mammoths and huge deer. Scientists have found tools that date back to about 12,000 years ago, when the glaciers were melting.

In the centuries that followed, most Native Americans of the Northwest relied on salmon from the Columbia River and Puget Sound to live. These fish were a staple of their diets. They were also the focus of Indian religious ceremonies.

In most parts of America, the only Indians who depended on fish lived on the coast. But because of the vastness of the Columbia River system and the habits of the salmon, inland tribes also depended on these big fish.

Opposite: Steamboat Rock and a grassy hillside

East of the Cascades, however, salmon were a special treat. Indians such as the Yakama, the Nez Perce, the Colville, and the Spokane trapped or netted salmon when the fish swam inland to breed. These Indians dried the fish in the sun to eat during winter. They also hunted deer and elk and gathered berries and roots.

The Makah, who still live on the northwestern tip of the Olympic Peninsula, fished for bigger game from the sea—whales. Today, they are the only people with government permission to hunt whales.

Early Exploration

Early explorers came to Washington by sea from several different lands. Sailors came from Spain, England, and Greece. They were

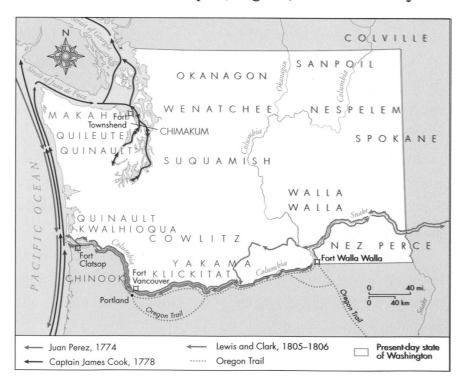

Exploration of Washington

← Juan Perez, 1774   ← Lewis and Clark, 1805–1806   ☐ Present-day state of Washington
← Captain James Cook, 1778   ······ Oregon Trail

all seeking a Northwest Passage that would somehow take them to the Far East.

One explorer whose Spanish name is on large bodies of water in western Washington was not Spanish and he may not even have actually explored the region. The maps call him Juan de Fuca. In fact, he was a Greek named Apostolos Valerianos. He claimed, many years later, to have entered the wide strait that separates Washington and Canada's Vancouver Island in 1592. When Charles Barkley, an American, sailed into that strait in 1787, he named it for Juan de Fuca.

In 1774, a Spanish explorer named Juan Perez sailed past the mouth of the Columbia River but did not notice it behind a curtain of mist. During the following years, some Spanish explorers from Mexico probably landed on the Olympic Peninsula, strengthening Spain's claim to the region.

Quinault Indians killed the first Spanish sailors who landed there. But Spain remained interested in the region. In about 1790, they built a fort-village on Neah Bay on the northern tip of the peninsula.

In 1778, Captain James Cook of Great Britain sailed along the coast. What he saw of the land and its wildlife made British traders and trappers head to the area for furs. But again, fog kept Washington veiled as Cook sailed past the Strait of Juan de Fuca.

Robert Gray was the American captain of a small ship called the *Columbia Redidiva*. In 1792, he sailed along the coast and saw the wide mouth of a river he could not find on any map. After sailing down the waterway, Captain Gray named it the Columbia River in honor of his vessel.

Captain James Cook sailed along the coast of what is now Washington.

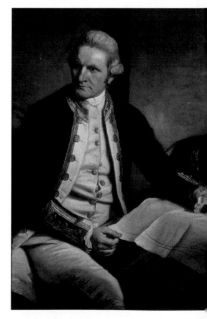

Captain George
Vancouver explored
Puget Sound.

One British captain, George Vancouver, explored Puget Sound, which he named for an officer aboard his ship. Certain that Captain Gray's river was really an inlet of the sea, Captain Vancouver sent a ship from his fleet to investigate. The captain of that ship found the river and claimed the land surrounding it for Britain.

Exploring from the Land

President Thomas Jefferson sent Meriwether Lewis and William Clark to explore the land the United States had bought from France in the Louisiana Purchase of 1803. After crossing the Continental Divide in the Rockies, the two explorers and their team canoed along the Clearwater River to the Snake River. They traveled on the Columbia from where it joined the Snake and reached the Columbia's mouth on November 15, 1805.

When they returned to St. Louis, Missouri, the following year, the expedition spread word of the wonders they had seen in the Northwest. In 1811, the Canadian Northwest Fur Company quietly explored the land and wildlife along the Columbia River in eastern Washington. They established a fur-trading post at Spokane. John

A Dramatic Start

Ross Cox, a member of the Astor expedition, became separated from the others and was left wandering in eastern Washington—on foot, without weapons, and without food. Two weeks later, he was close to death when he stumbled across some Indians. They took him to where they knew his party was busy building a fur-trading fort. When the Americans abandoned the region the following year, Cox, despite his frightening start, stayed behind. Eventually he wrote *Adventures on the Columbia River,* which told many exciting stories of life in the wilderness. ■

Jacob Astor's fur traders attempted to move into the same area, but their business ended when a supply ship that was supposed to bring food failed to arrive.

Fort Vancouver served as headquarters of Hudson's Bay Company.

Hudson's Bay Company had its headquarters at Fort Vancouver on the Columbia River. During the early 1800s, the fort was the social and business center of the entire Northwest. In its heyday, it had at least twenty-seven buildings and several hundred residents. As more Americans moved into the area to farm, the British company moved its headquarters to Vancouver Island.

Both Britain and the United States claimed the region, which was called Oregon Country. But the two countries were fighting the War of 1812 and couldn't reach final agreement on Oregon Country. The Treaty of Ghent ended the war in 1815. It gave both countries the right to the region south of the 54° 40' parallel for a period of ten years.

Puget Sound in the 1880s

The ten-year agreement was renewed twice. After 1836, things began to change. Families began arriving from across the Rockies. The first ones were missionaries to the Indians.

The Whitmans

Nathaniel Wyeth and William Sublette pioneered the Oregon Trail from the Missouri River to the Columbia River in 1832. However, they did it without wagons, using only pack mules.

In 1835, the Joint Congregational Presbyterian and Reformed Churches sent Dr. Marcus Whitman and Reverend Samuel Parker to Oregon Country. They went to find out about establishing a mission for the Nez Perce Indians. The prospects looked good, and they returned east to organize a permanent mission.

The following year, Whitman, along with his new bride, Narcissa Prentiss, and missionaries Henry and Eliza Spalding, set off with seventy rugged frontiersmen to try to cross the Rocky Mountains. Their supplies were carried in two large, heavy wagons. The guides told them that loaded wagons had never made it across the Continental Divide.

Marcus Whitman and his group at South Pass

Whitman was able to convince the disgruntled guides to help him get his supplies over the mountains. Narcissa Prentiss Whitman and Eliza Spalding became the first European women to cross the Continental Divide.

However, at the Snake River, the guides rebelled, refusing to take the wagons any farther. The missionaries had to abandon their wagons, taking only what their pack mules could carry. The Whitmans established their mission among the Cayuse people at Waiilatpu, now called Walla Walla.

Marcus and Narcissa Whitman spent eleven years at their mission. As missionaries, they were unsuccessful. Not a single Cayuse joined their church. However, they welcomed all the travelers, or emigrants, along the newly opened Oregon Trail.

Unfortunately, one settler brought measles to the mission. The disease spread immediately and killed fourteen Cayuse, including several children. The Indians blamed the missionaries for the deaths. They attacked and killed everyone at the mission, including Narcissa and Marcus Whitman. They also kidnapped the women and children, who were later ransomed by Peter Skene Ogden of the Hudson's Bay Company's Fort Vancouver.

Movement into the West

The first large groups to take the Oregon Trail headed to the Willamette Valley south of the Columbia River in present-day Oregon. But in 1845, the fertile land north of the river began to attract settlers who wanted to be American, not British.

By 1848, so many people had moved into the area that the U.S. government created Oregon Territory. Oregon Territory included what is now Washington, Oregon, Idaho, and the western parts of Montana and Wyoming.

Washington Territory was separated from Oregon Territory in 1853. Olympia was its capital. Ten years later, Idaho Territory was separated from Washington. In 1865, Montana Territory was formed, leaving Washington as we know it today.

The Nez Perce

The early fur trappers gave the Indians of southeastern Washington, northeastern Oregon, and central Idaho the name *Nez Perce*, which means "pierced nose" in French. Only a few of the Nez Perce actually wore shells in their noses, but the Shahaptian-speaking tribe was stuck with the name. ■

"Fifty-four Forty or Fight"

In the 1844 U.S. presidential election, the Democratic Party candidate James K. Polk used the slogan "Fifty-four Forty or Fight." Polk wanted the United States to take the entire region south of latitude 54° 40', called Oregon Country. However, in 1846, diplomats established a new northern border between Canada and the United States at latitude 49°, the forty-ninth parallel, more than 350 miles (563 km) to the south. In a later compromise, the United States gave up its claims to Vancouver Island. The island then became part of British Columbia. ■

Washington Territory

Isaac I. Stevens was the first governor of Washington Territory.

President Millard Fillmore appointed an engineer-soldier named Isaac I. Stevens as the first territorial governor of Washington Territory. Fillmore also appointed him superintendent of Indian affairs. The first territorial election was held on January 30, 1854. The legislature met a month later.

Stevens's main task as territorial governor was to regain Native American lands. He made unfair treaties with many different tribes. The United States got their land, and the Indians were forced to move onto reservations. The U.S. Senate never approved some of Stevens's treaties, however, and some settlers moved onto Indian land illegally.

More than 17,000 Indians gave up their right to more than

64 million acres (26 million hectares) of land. Some tribes kept fishing rights, which they still use.

Chief Sealth (whose name settlers later pronounced *Seattle*) was a Salish Indian living on Bainbridge Island. He was a friend of a settler named David Maynard, who lived in Olympia. At Sealth's urging, Maynard moved to the place known as Duwamps. In 1855, Sealth signed the treaty that gave the land around Puget Sound to the United States. Maynard changed the name of Duwamps to Seattle, after his friend.

Eastern Washington's open rangeland first drew cattle ranchers to the area. In Washington Territory's early days, a cattle-drive route called the Cariboo Trail went from the Dalles in Oregon up into British Columbia in Canada. In the 1850s and 1860s, the cattle were used to feed the gold miners in the Fraser River area. When this profitable market ran out of gold, sheep became the main livestock of this open land, often called the Big Bend Plateau.

David Maynard named the city of Seattle after Cheif Sealth.

Chief Sealth's Speech

During a meeting with Territorial Governor Isaac I. Stevens, Chief Sealth is said to have given a dramatic speech about the plight of his tribe. No one recorded the chief's exact words, but one man's memory of it was published in 1887. However, the chief spoke in Salish, so the published memories may have been made up.

According to legend, the old chief said, "It matters little where we pass the remnant of our days. They will not be many. The Indian's night promises to be dark. Not a single star of hope hovers above his horizon. Sad-voiced winds moan in the distance. Grim fate seems to be on the Red Man's trail, and wherever he will hear the approaching footsteps of his fell destroyer and prepare stolidly to meet his doom, as does the wounded doe that hears the approaching footsteps of the hunter." ■

Historical map of Washington

When farmers tried to settle this region, they found that the soil was too shallow for crops. Only the valleys, where rivers flowed, had enough moisture and soil for agriculture, and such places were limited.

Gold was discovered near Colville in the northeastern part of Washington. Gold hunters paid no attention to treaties, so war soon broke out against the Yakama Indians. Native Americans, settlers, Territorial Governor Stevens, a territorial supreme court judge, and local soldiers all became involved in the Yakama Indian War, which lasted three years. It ended in 1858 with a Yakama defeat at the Battle of Four Lakes. Several Indian chiefs were executed.

Chief Joseph

In-mut-too-yah-lat-lat was a Nez Perce leader. The settlers called him Chief Joseph. He led the struggle of Native Americans to live in eastern Washington. In 1877, the U.S. government ordered the Nez Perce to give up their land and move to a small reservation. During the forced move, Nez Perce warriors killed several white settlers.

Knowing they would be blamed, Chief Joseph and other chiefs fled eastward. Soldiers followed them and the brief Nez Perce War took place. Chief Joseph surrendered at the Battle of Bear Paw Mountain and was sent into exile in Indian Territory. In 1885, Chief Joseph and some of his followers were allowed to go to Colville Reservation in Washington.

In 1903, a year before his death, Chief Joseph became a celebrity when he went to Washington, D.C., to plead his cause. Today, the Nez Perce reservation is in Idaho. ■

After Congress finally ratified all the treaties, white settlers were free to go almost anywhere they wanted. It was the Native Americans who had lost out.

The Growing Land

Fewer than 4,000 settlers lived in Washington when it separated from Oregon Territory in 1853. By the time it became a state in 1889, it had a population of 357,000, considerably more than was needed for statehood.

The first transcontinental railroad opened in 1869. It went from Nebraska to Sacramento, California, but its route left the Northwest still isolated. Finally, in 1883, tracks of the Northern Pacific

The railroads brought new settlers to Washington and enabled the timber industry to grow.

Railroad and the Oregon Railway and Navigation Company met up, creating a new northern route. Thousands of settlers then poured into Washington. Between 1880 and 1920, the state's population multiplied more than fifteen times, largely because of the railroads.

Washington's Native Americans had not been settled on their reservations long when Congress passed an act taking the land away again. The Dawes Act of 1887 forced individual Indians to choose their own 160-acre (65-ha) plots. White settlers were then allowed to choose their own land on what had been the reservations. This private ownership of land contradicted Native American tradition and marked the end of many aspects of tribal life.

In the last years before statehood, sections of eastern Washington were flooded with settlers. By then, wheat was the most important crop. The southeast corner of the state was almost completely planted within just a few short years. It offered a better climate for growing crops than other parts of the region.

The northeastern corner of the state wasn't settled so readily. The railroad there—the Northern Pacific—stopped at the Grand Coulee of the Columbia River. A *coulee* is a valley with very steep sides jutting upward from a river.

Half a million bushels of wheat waiting for shipment

Most people thought that the Grand Coulee would never be crossed.

In the meantime, farmers in the southeast had to take their produce to Spokane to ship it out. That city grew as the capital of what came to be called the Inland Empire. It was the only city of any importance between Minneapolis/St. Paul in Minnesota and Seattle.

The territory had fewer than 24,000 residents in the 1870 census, but toward the end of the decade, they were certain they had the 40,000 people necessary to become a state. They wrote and submitted a constitution for congressional approval in 1878, but it was rejected. Washingtonians continued to submit constitutional drafts during the next few years.

Finally, within a few months in the late 1880s, the U.S. Congress admitted six states to the Union. Washington, the forty-second state, was admitted to the Union on November 11, 1889.

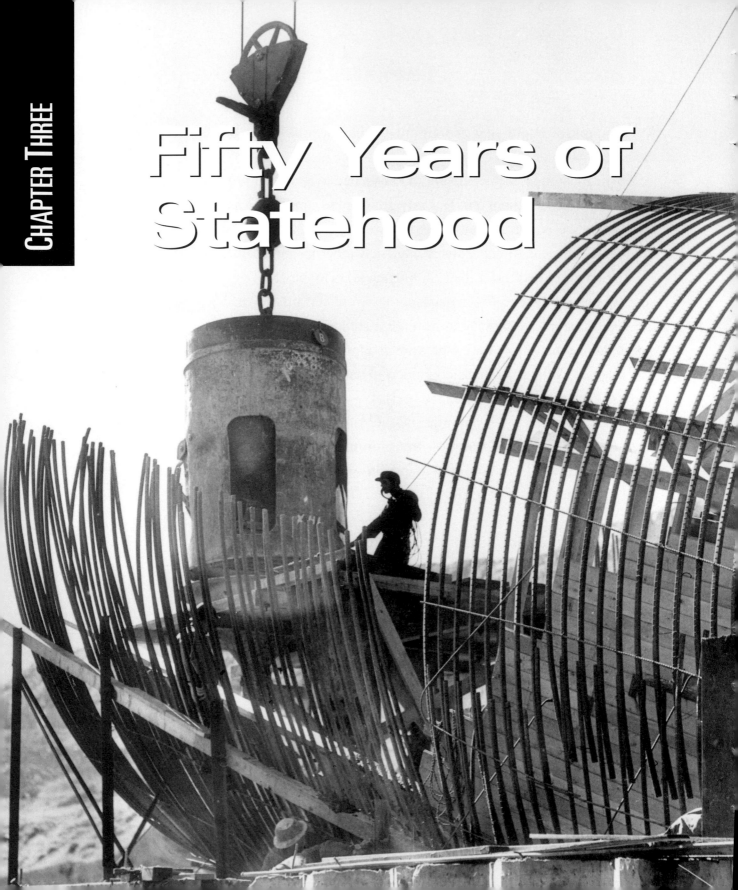

CHAPTER THREE

Fifty Years of Statehood

When Washingtonians approved the new state's constitution in 1889, they also elected the first state governor—Elisha P. Ferry. He took the oath of office in Olympia one week after statehood was declared.

Olympia was still an undeveloped town. It wasn't until 1892 that a major building, the county courthouse, was constructed. That building was the state capitol from 1901 until 1928, when a new one was completed. The new capitol is called the Legislative Building.

Washington had been a state only a few years when a major economic depression hit the United States. Many of the thriving young state's new businesses closed in the Panic of 1893. The lumber business in particular suffered, until the Klondike gold rush of 1897 brought prosperity to the Northwest again.

The state's big business in Washington's early years was timber. Companies used steam engines to carry big logs out of the forests. All the other wood was left to rot and burn. The skies over Washington were often filled with smoke.

Gifford Pinchot, chief of President Theodore Roosevelt's new U.S. Forest Service, began to introduce forest conservation. He called for fire protection in the forests and lower taxes on forestland.

Elisha P. Ferry was the first governor of the state of Washington.

Opposite: Construction of the Grand Coulee Dam

The Growing State

By the time Washington became a state in 1889, the steamships that traveled the major rivers of the eastern part of the state had given way to three railway lines. This allowed the region's farms to get their produce to the nation's major markets. Everett became the terminal of the Great Northern Railway. Over the next twenty years, the railway brought thousands of European immigrants to Washington as the result of a worldwide advertising campaign. By 1910, the state had more than 1 million residents.

The growth of Seattle occurred because of a discovery far to the north of Puget Sound. Gold was discovered in 1896 along the Klondike River in western Canada.

On July 17, 1897, a steamship from the north arrived in Seattle. In addition to its passengers, it carried gold. An estimated 70,000 of the 100,000 gold hunters who rushed to the Klondike went through Seattle. The merchants of Seattle earned more than the gold hunters did.

Shipping that had previously gone to San Francisco began to head for Seattle, and the city became a major port. Four railroads were built to Seattle. Because the city needed wood to grow and wood was also shipped to points south and east, the lumber business in Seattle boomed.

Lumber being loaded for shipment

The Evolving Land

The western timber-growing part of the state was settled early on. By 1889, the eastern, wheat-growing region was pretty well settled, too. But with little usable water, the central part of the state was almost a no-man's-land. Cattle raising was about the only agricultural activity there.

People urged the government to do something about the problem. That "something" was to irrigate the land by building dams on the rivers that fed into the Columbia. At that time, dams on the Columbia were merely a dream—it was too difficult to get the water up from the deep valley through which it ran.

The Northern Pacific Railroad, knowing that it would have an easier time selling irrigated land, began to dig canals from the Yakima River and its tributaries. The Great Northern Railway did the same from the Wenatchee to the Okanogan. The railroads, and then the government, also began to build reservoirs to store water for use in those periods when the rivers were at their lowest.

By 1910, the whole Yakima region was irrigated farmland. However, the land was so costly that farmers could buy only a little of it. They had to grow smaller crops that were sent directly to market instead of large crops sold to wholesalers. Fruit orchards became the most economical crop for these small farms. "Apple fever" took over eastern Washington.

Apples became an important crop for Washington.

Alaska-Yukon-Pacific Exposition, Seattle, June 1 to October 16, 1909

Third Annual Rose Festival,
Portland, June 7 to 12, 1909

Yellowstone Park,
Season June 5 to Sept. 25, 1909

Form a trinity of attractions which will outrival any heretofore offered. With efficient train service afforded, each of these may be visited in one transcontinental tour and Yellowstone Park entered through

Gardiner Gateway
the official entrance. Three modern electric-lighted trains daily (after May 23rd) in each direction between St. Paul - Minneapolis, and one train daily between Missouri River points and the North Pacific Coast. Through Pullmans to the Coast and to the Park boundary.

Send for travel literature—furnished free.

Northern Pacific Railway
A. M. Cleland, General Passenger Agent
St. Paul, Minn.

The Northern Pacific Railway tried to lure people to events in Washington as well as other states in the Northwest.

Celebrating Growth

In 1909, a huge fair in Seattle was planned to celebrate the economic growth of the entire northwestern part of North America. The Alaska-Yukon-Pacific Exposition celebrated the fact that Seattle and Puget Sound were tied to the Klondike and the Territory of Alaska. The Fair in the Forest took place on the forested grounds of the University of Washington. When planning began, the university had only three buildings. Four large buildings added for the fair later became a permanent part of the attractive university campus.

Some 90,000 people attended the opening ceremonies of the Alaska-Yukon-Pacific Exposition. Nearly 4 million people attended the fair during its run. Most visitors were amazed to discover that Seattle was a booming, cultured city, not a frontier outpost. Audiences enjoyed many exhibits, including a demonstration of the forerunner of radio.

Wobblies and War

The timber industry and railroads were the biggest contributors to Washington's growth. Both industries employed a great many workers. As a result, Washington became an important center for the labor-union movement.

At the turn of the century, many Chinese were making a living in the West. But some of the white newcomers in the region wanted the jobs that the Chinese held. They began to riot against the Chinese. In Washington, such riots occurred in mining camps and fruit orchards.

As the world was discovering Seattle, Washingtonians were dealing with labor riots, demonstrations, and strikes. The Industrial Workers of the World, often referred to as Wobblies, sometimes used sabotage, rather than political action, to improve working conditions for laborers.

The Wobblies were more successful in the mines, lumber camps, and farms of the Northwest than anywhere else. However, they lost a lot of support when they opposed the United States' entry into World War I (1914–1918). The U.S. government prosecuted some of the group's leaders.

America's involvement in World War I began in 1917. Camp Lewis (later called Fort Lewis) became an important training

The Everett Massacre

In November 1916, a group of Wobblies was thrown out of the lumber town of Everett. When an even larger group took a ferry back into Everett, the businessmen of the town gathered at the dock to prevent them from landing. Shots were fired. Within minutes, seven people were dead and at least fifty were injured. All seventy-five people who were arrested were later released, but people remained bitter about the Everett Massacre. ■

Men arriving for training at Camp Lewis in 1917

center for the U.S. Army. With huge naval shipyards at Bremerton, the southern part of Puget Sound also played a vital role.

As the war was ending in 1918, the Wobblies' efforts ended terribly. Some union members in Centralia were in their hall when a group of angry American legion members broke in. The Wobblies killed four legion members. The other legion members then captured a Wobbly and hung him. The lynching stunned America.

The Great Depression

In 1929, the New York Stock Exchange crashed. Timber sales in the Northwest dropped drastically as new building was discontinued all over the country. Farm prices fell. Everywhere, people lost their jobs and couldn't find work.

In 1932, Democrat Franklin D. Roosevelt was elected president. He promised to rescue the United States from the Great Depression with his New Deal programs. He persuaded Congress to use federal money to establish projects in various states that would put people to work.

One of Washington's projects was the creation of Olympic National Park in 1938. The new 648,000-acre (262,000-ha) park was controversial. Paper and pulp companies insisted they needed the western hemlock trees on the peninsula to keep people working. When Roosevelt added one-third more acreage to the park four years later, any expansion of the paper industry in the area was essentially ended.

President Roosevelt and his group viewing the Bonneville Dam on the Columbia River in 1937

Japanese Internment

After the Japanese attack on Pearl Harbor in Hawaii in 1941, many Americans began to fear Japanese—and Japanese Americans—people living in the United States. In February 1942, concerned about keeping the peace, President Franklin D. Roosevelt ordered all people of Japanese descent out of regions in the country where the war effort was going on. The government took thousands of Japanese Americans to an assembly center in Puyallup and then to camps primarily in California and Idaho. They were held in the camps, like prisoners of war, for the rest of the war. ■

Roosevelt also promised to build two dams on the Columbia River. The Grand Coulee, in central Washington, would irrigate the area for agriculture. The Bonneville Dam, just east of Portland, Oregon, would generate electric power. The dams were built, but World War II (1939–1945) changed their purposes. All available electricity was needed to power the war industry.

World War II

America's involvement in World War II began on December 7, 1941, when Japan bombed Pearl Harbor in Hawaii. Most Washingtonians feared that their state, too, would become a target for Japan's bombers.

The Boeing Company, an airplane manufacturer in Seattle, looked particularly vulnerable. Workers camouflaged the plant by covering it with canvas cloth painted with trees and houses and lawns to look like an open suburban area from the air. The people who lived around Puget Sound were ordered to hang blackout curtains in their homes so that no light would be visible at night to direct bombers to a target. However, when it became clear that the Japanese were busy elsewhere, Puget Sounders relaxed.

Boeing built many planes during World War II.

During the war, power generated by the Columbia River's dams was put to major industrial use for the first time. Manufacturers used the power supply to turn bauxite ore into aluminum. Huge aluminum mills were built in Tacoma, Longview, and Spokane. Soon almost half of the nation's supply of the metal was coming from Washington.

Seattle enjoyed massive growth during the war because of the Boeing Company, which employed more than 50,000 workers. The company's major job was building the B-17 bomber, an important fighting plane used by the United States during World War II.

In Vancouver and neighboring Portland, the Henry J. Kaiser firm used power from Bonneville Dam for shipbuilding. Kaiser built more than 140 ships during World War II, mostly the quickly constructed Liberty ships that kept supplies moving to Europe throughout the war.

About twice the number of Boeing employees worked in the shipyards of Puget Sound. The region's population ballooned. Many of the new workers were African-Americans.

The Manhattan Project

All over the country, the government warned people not to talk about their war work because it might help the enemy. But nothing was kept as secret as the Manhattan Project in south-central Washington. The Manhattan Project was a top-secret, high-level effort to produce an atomic bomb. As part of the Manhattan Project, a 1,000-square-mile (2,590-square-kilometer) chunk of central Washington became the Hanford Site, where restricted activities went on. Many people who worked at Hanford didn't even know exactly what the project was.

Thousands of people were brought in to design, build, and operate the first nuclear reactor. Its job was to process the fairly plentiful uranium 238 into the very rare uranium 235. That type of uranium was then converted to plutonium 239. The atoms of plutonium can be split and exploded with unimaginable force. This was the material needed for the atomic bomb.

The first bomb was tested at Alamagordo, New Mexico, in July 1945. The results were more powerful than anyone had imagined.

A Washington Newsman

News broadcaster Edward R. Murrow lived in Washington much of his life. He kept Americans informed about World War II news on the radio. Born Egbert Murrow in North Carolina in 1908, Murrow went to high school in Bellingham and attended Washington State College in Pullman. He worked summers in logging camps. He began working for the Columbia Broadcasting System (CBS) in 1935. CBS sent him to Europe in 1937. Most Americans listened to his regular broadcasts from England, as bombs fell around him. They trusted him to tell the truth.

After the war, Murrow was a CBS executive and created the history series *You Are There*. He preferred to be on the air, however. He continued to work as a broadcaster, interviewing famous people on *Person to Person*. President John F. Kennedy made Murrow director of the U.S. Information Agency, an organization that aired government broadcasts throughout the world. Murrow died in 1965, but his fame has never faded. ■

Only a few weeks later, President Harry S. Truman approved the first use of the atomic bomb in warfare. He decided that invading Japan would kill too many U.S. soldiers, so he chose to drop the atomic bomb on Hiroshima, Japan, instead. A few days later, when Japan had not yet surrendered, a second bomb was dropped on Nagasaki. The Japanese then agreed to surrender, and World War II was over.

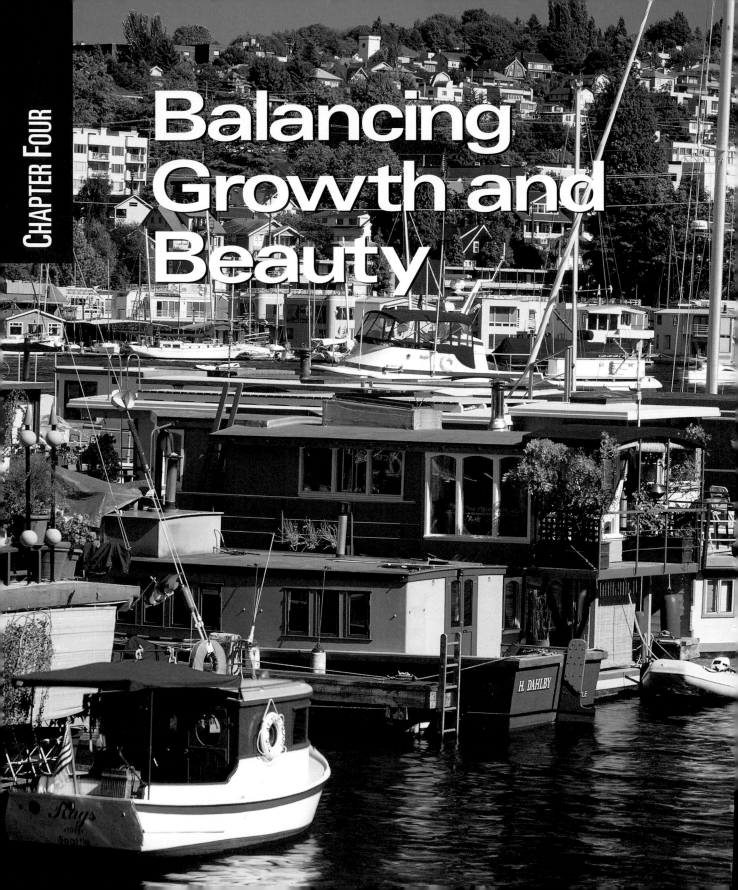

CHAPTER FOUR

Balancing Growth and Beauty

After World War II, Washington State grew rapidly. The growth was a result of the availability of cheap power and a growing appreciation for the state's beauty. Unfortunately, much of the growth occurred without any planning or zoning laws, and many beautiful places were lost forever.

Within just a few short years, Lake Washington turned into a polluted cesspool. Development around the lake grew rapidly without adequate plans for waste disposal. It took the creation of a new council with representatives from Seattle and all other towns on Lake Washington to eventually clean up the lake.

In the mid-1950s, a group of businessmen met to plan an anniversary celebration of the 1909 Alaska-Yukon-Pacific Exposition in Seattle. Their simple plan gradually turned into the world's fair of 1962. They took the opportunity to rebuild the core of Seattle. The centerpiece of the 74-acre (30-ha) fair was the Space

Due to efforts by concerned citizens, Lake Washington's beauty has been restored.

Opposite: Houseboats on Lake Union

Crowds enjoying the world's fair of 1962

Needle, a futuristic symbol of the fair's theme—Century 21.

Between April 21 and October 21, 1962, millions visited Seattle. Preparation for the fair had produced a refurbished city with several new cultural sites and a new transportation system. By the time Century 21 took place, people could swim and fish in Lake Washington.

Unfortunately, other parts of the state were in danger. In his 1960 book *My Wilderness: The Pacific West*, U.S. Supreme Court justice William O. Douglas wrote about the loss of a favorite meadow on Mount Adams: "I have seen in my lifetime a wilderness of trails remade into a maze of roads. . . . The network of roads is so vast and intricate that almost every wilderness area is threatened."

In 1966, Governor Daniel Evans asked, "How can our state grow with grace?" It was a tough question with no easy answer.

Minorities in Washington

African-Americans had lived in western Washington since the founding of its major cities. William Grose was a Seattle landowner. Horace Cayton was the publisher of a Seattle newspaper. However, when more black people began to move into Seattle and Tacoma during the Great Depression, and later during World War II, they weren't always welcomed.

Things were no different east of the Cascades. The DuPont Company built segregated housing for the black workers at Hanford, and their children went to separate schools. It took the civil rights movement of the 1960s to change things.

After World War II, Hispanics outnumbered African-Americans in the state. Thousands had come to eastern Washington to replace field-workers who had left to fight in the war. The United States and Mexico agreed that Mexicans could come to America temporarily. After the war, many Hispanic laborers came to Washington from other states.

When the civil rights movement began, many Washingtonians assumed that it had nothing to do with them. However, a radical organization called the Black Panthers held demonstrations that turned violent in Seattle and Tacoma. Most of the city school districts worked out desegregation policies before the courts ordered them.

In the late 1960s, people in Washington protested against American involvement in the Vietnam War. One notorious group called the Seattle Seven broke into Seattle's federal courthouse. They were tried and sent to prison.

Washington in Space

After World War II ended and orders for military aircraft tapered off, the Boeing Company fired 75 percent of its workforce. Washingtonians realized that their economic health depended on one company. However, the Cold War—the continuing political con-

Boeing played a part in creating the Saturn V, the biggest rocket ever built.

flict between the Soviet Union and the United States—meant that Boeing and Hanford continued to be important.

In the early 1960s, the National Aeronautics and Space Administration (NASA) gave Boeing a contract to build part of the Saturn V rocket. This rocket launched astronauts to the moon in the Apollo program of the late 1960s and early 1970s. Thousands of people were put to work on the project.

The Mystery of D. B. Cooper

On November 24, 1971, a man calling himself Dan Cooper bought an airline ticket from Portland, Oregon, to Seattle. As the plane was taking off, he informed the flight attendant that he had a bomb in his briefcase and was hijacking the airplane. He demanded $200,000, two chest parachutes, and two back parachutes in exchange for the passengers' freedom.

He got his wish and kept his promise. With one flight attendant on board, he ordered the plane to take off again from Seattle. He strapped the money, which authorities had marked, in a belt around his waist and strapped on the parachutes. He ordered the pilot to head south slowly toward Reno, Nevada. Thirty-seven minutes after takeoff, the

hijacker lowered the aircraft's stairs and jumped.

For weeks, the mysterious D. B. Cooper and his ill-gotten money were hunted throughout the Cascades. He was never found. In 1980, picnickers near Vancouver found three packets of the marked money. The rest has never shown up. The story remains one of Washington's great mysteries. ■

Boeing is now the main contractor for the space shuttle flight program. The company is also building a major part of the International Space Station and manages the integration of the sections built by other countries for NASA. The Boeing plant in Everett focuses on building commercial aircraft.

Beyond the Mountains

Eastern Washington has flourished since the building of the Grand Coulee Dam. The dam's irrigation water and electric power changed the entire region, which had been isolated and economically disadvantaged.

Not to be outdone by the western side of the state, Spokane held Expo '74, its own world's fair, in 1974. With little more than 150,000 people at the time, Spokane was the smallest city ever to stage a world's fair. Like Seattle, Spokane cleaned up its water—the Spokane River, where miners had dumped waste for decades—in time for the fair.

The 1974 world's fair in Spokane

Native Americans and Fish

In the 1850s, Territorial Governor Isaac I. Stevens signed treaties allowing various Indian tribes to keep their right to fish. Stevens thought these rights had no real importance. But fifty years later, commercial fishing had become a huge business on Puget Sound. Gradually the fish stocks shrank. Commercial fishing suffered. And environmentalists fought to preserve the fish, especially five salmon species that had begun to disappear when the dams were built.

After World War II, Indians began fighting back for their rights. They used techniques from the civil rights movement, such as sit-ins. One Native American named Billy Frank Jr. went to jail ninety times during the struggle to retain fishing rights. But little was settled until the federal government sided with the Native Americans against the state of Washington.

In 1974, federal judge George Boldt declared that the treaties were valid. He confirmed the right of Native Americans to fish where and however they had traditionally fished. The U.S. Supreme Court backed Boldt's decision. Suddenly, white commercial fishermen were fighting Indian fishermen. At the start of the twenty-first century, the two groups were trying to find ways to cope with the shrinking fish supply.

Hanford's Nuclear Power

When enough plutonium had been stockpiled for future use, the government wanted to close Hanford's reactors. Washington State wanted to convert one of the reactors so it would produce electricity. However, throughout the United States, coal-mine owners, railroads

Mount St. Helens

Mount St. Helens, south of Tacoma on the edge of Gifford Pinchot National Forest, was famed for its beautiful shape—a single, isolated volcanic mountain that resembled Japan's famous Mount Fuji. Long thought to be dormant, the mountain suddenly erupted violently on May 18, 1980. More than 1,300 feet (397 m) of its top slid into the valley below, causing a weak spot through which lava blasted side-ways. Fifty-seven people died. Almost 150,000 acres (60,750 ha) of forest were blasted down.

In 1982, President Ronald Reagan set aside 110,000 acres (45,000 ha) around the mountain as Mount St. Helens National Volcanic Monument. Two interpretation and visitors centers were established, and visitors are now allowed to climb to the summit of the mountain again. ■

that carried coal, and power companies that burned coal objected to the scheme. They were afraid it would hurt their industries. Finally, Senator Henry Jackson of Washington suggested that the power companies receive half of all the power Hanford produced.

A group of small electric-power companies formed the Washington Public Power Supply System (WPPSS) to build huge power plants. But by 1982, only one of the five planned nuclear reactors was built and functioning. The WPPSS collapsed and its mammoth cooling towers still stand unused.

Gradually, as Hanford shut down, the nearby Tri-Cities area of Richland, Pasco, and Kennewick had to find a new basis for its economy. People had to find ways to stimulate their businesses. New private industry was brought to the area. Dry land was irrigated, and crops were planted.

By the end of the twentieth century, radioactive-waste storage tanks in the ground at Hanford were beginning to leak. Some of the leakage was only 400 yards (366 meters) away from the Columbia

River. Some tumbleweed plants and water-breeding insects there have recently been found to be radioactive.

In 2000, Hanford became the largest environmental cleanup project ever. Experts predict that cleaning up the contamination will take many years and cost $50 billion.

The Spotted Owl

One small owl had a profound effect on Washington in the 1990s. The northern spotted owl lives and breeds only in the treetops of old-growth forests. Each pair of owls needs 100 acres (41 ha) to breed. Environmentalists wanted to ban the cutting of old-growth forests. Lumber companies argued against such a ban, claiming that the economies of Washington and Oregon would suffer.

In 1990, however, the U.S. Fish and Wildlife Service listed the northern spotted owl as an endangered species. It banned logging within 2,000 acres (810 ha) of a known owl nest. Although the decision was fought in court, the Supreme Court ultimately upheld it. The ban hit Washington communities that depended on logging hard.

In the first years after the decision, many towns in logging areas, particularly on the Olympic Peninsula, had serious economic troubles. Logging families were forced to move or find other ways to make a living. Recent improvements in forest management have brought logging back, however.

A New World

Writers Robert E. Ficken and Charles P. LeWarne wrote a history of Washington for the state's centennial in 1989. They reflected on the comfortable lifestyle of Washingtonians. The book ended with

The spotted owl has been the subject of much controversy in Washington.

these words: "As they reach their centennial year, Washingtonians might ponder from whence they came and whether the 'good life' is enough to sustain their future." What the authors didn't know was that a whole new way of sustaining the "good life" was already brewing.

It began in 1978 when two young men from Seattle—Bill Gates and Paul Allen—moved their young company back to Bellevue, a suburb of Seattle, from New Mexico. The incredible success of their company, called Microsoft, has drawn many other computer companies to Seattle. Some former Microsoft employees have also formed their own companies in the area. These people seek the best of both worlds—economic prosperity and protection of the state's natural beauty.

The Seattle area is home to many successful businesses.

CHAPTER FIVE

Two States in One

The Evergreen State is the farthest north and farthest west of the first forty-eight states. It is the twentieth-largest state, occupying 70,637 square miles (182,950 sq km). Its highest point, at 14,410 feet (4,395 m), is Mount Rainier in the Cascade Mountains. Its lowest point is sea level on the Pacific Ocean.

Washington borders British Columbia and the Strait of Georgia.

On the east, Washington is bordered by the narrow northern part of Idaho. Oregon lies to the south, and the Pacific Ocean lies to the west.

The northern border of Washington is part of the northern border of the United States. This border with the Canadian province of British Columbia follows the forty-ninth parallel until it hits the Strait of Georgia. Then the border jogs south around Canada's Vancouver Island.

A tiny tip of a peninsula belonging to British Columbia dips southward to a few miles below the forty-ninth parallel. This peninsula, called Point Roberts, belongs to the United States.

The Trembling Earth

Earth's crust is made up of huge sections called tectonic plates. Western Washington rides on the Juan de Fuca Plate. The much-larger North American Plate is slowly overriding it. The line

Opposite: Mount Rainier National Park

Liberty Bell Mountain in the Cascades

where the two plates come together is a region of great seismic activity. The Cascade Mountains are the result of the pressure between the two plates folding Earth's crust upward. Slips and slides where these two plates meet cause earthquakes. Also, molten lava from deep inside Earth sometimes escapes between the plates as volcanic eruptions.

Earthquakes of various sizes are felt somewhere in Washington every few weeks. The largest recorded earthquake in Washington occurred in 1872, but there are few reports about what happened. Most quakes do little more than shatter windows and occasionally break water mains.

However, with western Washington growing in population, earthquakes are an increasing concern. Many scientists feel that Washington, like California, is due for a major earthquake.

Fourteen volcanoes in the Cascade Mountains are possibly active. Before it erupted in 1980, Mount St. Helens had long been thought to be dormant, or not likely to erupt. North of Mount St. Helens, Mount Rainier has a history of eruptions, most recently in the 1840s. Based on its past history, Mount Rainier is likely to erupt again. Unfortunately, some heavily populated areas lie within the range of lava flow.

Washington's Geographical Features

Total area; rank	70,637 sq. mi. (182,950 sq km); 19th
Land; rank	66,581 sq. mi. (172,445 sq km); 20th
Water; rank	4,056 sq. mi. (10,505 sq km); 9th
Inland water; **rank**	1,545 sq. mi. (4,002 sq km); 14th
Coastal water; **rank**	2,511 sq. mi. (6,503 sq km); 2nd
Geographic center	Chelan, 10 miles (16 km) southwest of Wenatchee
Highest point	Mount Rainier, 14,410 feet (4,395 m)
Lowest point	Sea level along the coast
Largest city	Seattle
Population; rank	4,887,941 (1990 census); 18th
Record high temperature	118°F (48°C) in Grant County on July 24, 1928, and at Ice Harbor Dam on August 5, 1961
Record low temperature	–48°F (–44°C) at Mazama and Winthrop on December 30, 1968
Average July temperature	66°F (19°C)
Average January temperature	30°F (–1°C)
Average annual precipitation	38 inches (97 cm)

Mount St. Helens

Most Americans were taken completely by surprise when Mount St. Helens erupted on May 18, 1980. The sideways blast of the eruption caused a sonic boom that could be heard in Canada. The lava and rock ejected by the blast roared out at 450 miles (724 km) an hour, destroying everything in its path. In all, 57 people died, and 27 bridges, 221 houses, 185 miles (298 km) of road, and 17 miles (27 km) of railroad track were lost. Millions of trees were blasted into toothpicks. The destruction continued for 17 miles (27 km) from the center of the explosion.

The ash from the volcano silted up nearby rivers, changing the ecology of the region. However, within a month, natural vegetation

Trees and other plants have started to grow in areas devastated by Mount St. Helens' eruption.

began to appear above the dense ash that covered the land away from the volcano itself. It took many more months for persistent growth to show above the several-feet-deep ash closer to Mount St. Helens. Roosevelt elk began to migrate back into the region within months after the eruption.

The Mountains

The main mountains of Washington are in the Cascade Range. This range of mountains divides the state in half. The Cascade Range is high, with many individual peaks reaching 9,000 feet (2,745 m). The Cascades have only six passes, most of which were not discovered until long after settlers first arrived.

These mountains determine the physical character of Washington's two halves. East of the Cascades, the state is dry and fairly flat, though there are many hills and lower mountains. Parts of the land are so dry that it is considered desert. West of the Cascades, the state is very different. The area is wet and green. The Olympic Peninsula also boasts one of the most northern rain forests in the world.

The Olympic Mountains on the Olympic Peninsula and the Willapa Hills south of them continue to be formed as Earth's crust folds when the tectonic plates move. The Blue Mountains in the southeast, named for their color when seen from a distance, are older and lower than the Cascades.

National Parks

Washington has three mountainous national parks. They are the Olympic, Mount Rainier, and North Cascades National Parks.

In 1899, Mount Rainier National Park was founded as the nation's fifth national park. It covers 235,612 acres (95,423 ha) of the Cascade Range. Mount Rainier, approximately in the center of the Cascade Range, has three summits that are remnants of previous eruptions. The highest is Columbia Crest, an area of more than 35 square miles (91 sq km) at the top of the mountain is made up of glaciers, permanent ice, and snow. One glacier extends all the

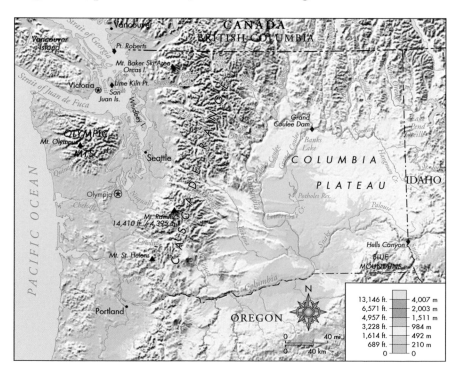

Washington's topography

Mount Baker covered in snow

way down to an elevation of 3,500 feet (1,068 m), making it one of the lowest glaciers in the United States.

North Cascades National Park, founded in 1968, covers more than 500,000 acres (202,500 ha). It is a land of ice. The park's centerpieces are Mount Baker and Mount Shuksan. The taller Mount Baker gets more snow than anywhere else on Earth. Rain, fog, mist, and snow contribute to the mountain's snowfields and glaciers. About two-thirds of all glaciers located in the lower forty-eight states are found in this park and the surrounding wilderness areas.

Olympic National Park occupies the heart of the Olympic Peninsula plus a 62-mile (100-km) coastal strip. Washington is famous for this spectacular temperate rain forest. It has the same heavy, always damp, almost jungle atmosphere of a tropical rain forest, but it is much farther north of course. Mosses hang on tree limbs, and giant fungi spread across the ground.

The rain forest exists because the Olympic Mountains, in the middle of the peninsula, are high enough to trap moisture-laden clouds from the ocean and force them to drop their water on the western side of the mountains. That makes the San Juan Islands, farther east, quite dry.

The highest peak in Olympic National Park is Mount Olympus, named after a mountain in Greece. It is 7,965 feet (2,429 m) high. Many elk live in the area around Mount Olympus. In order to protect them, President Theodore Roosevelt declared the area a national monument in 1909. In 1939, the area became the core of Olympic National Park's 922,651 acres (373,674 ha).

Olympic National Park is moist and green.

The Forests

Washington was nicknamed the Evergreen State because so much of its land was covered with evergreen, coniferous trees, such as western hemlock, western red cedar, Sitka spruce, ponderosa and lodgepole pine, and yew. Most of these trees are very tall. Douglas firs can grow 300 feet (92 m) high. Only the sequoias of California are taller.

Washington's forests are the largest remaining forests in the United States. It is estimated that they occupy 36,000 square miles (93,240 sq km)—about as much land as there is in Indiana!

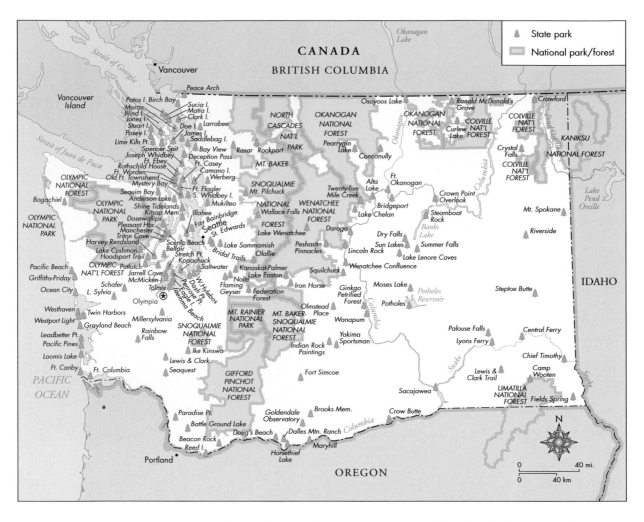

Washington's parks and forests

Six national forests are located entirely in Washington—Colville, Gifford Pinchot, Mount Baker-Snoqualmie, Okanogan, Olympic, and Wenatchee. Washington shares Umatilla National Forest with Oregon, and Kaniksu with Idaho and Montana.

Evergreens are not the only wonderful plant life in Washington. There are many broad-leaved trees whose early spring growth creates a haze of green in the landscape. In the autumn, those same trees turn colors as spectacular as any trees in New England.

Rhododendron bushes, which produce the state flower, grow

throughout the damp part of Washington. These evergreen bushes come in many varieties. The mountains and valleys colored with many varieties of wildflowers are a delightful place to hike in spring and summer.

The Coast

Only about 150 miles (241 km) of the west side of Washington is on the Pacific Ocean, but the state has considerably more shoreline. The Strait of Juan de Fuca, south of Vancouver Island, and the Strait of Georgia, east of Vancouver, are tidal shore. The complex system of waterways called Puget Sound is also tidal shore. That contributes to Washington's more than 3,000 miles (4,827 km) of shoreline. No wonder the shores are just as important to outdoor living as the mountains.

Adding considerably to the miles of shoreline are the San Juan Islands in the Strait of Georgia and down into Puget Sound. When the tide from the Pacific Ocean is out, almost 800 rocks and land-

Fall colors in Colville National Forest

masses can be called islands. When the tide comes in, nearly 200 of them remain visible. These islands were left above the water level more than 12,000 years ago when the great glaciers retreated. The three largest islands—San Juan, Orcas, and Lopez—have the most residents.

San Juan Island itself represents 57 square miles (148 sq km) of leisurely living. Lime Kiln Point on this island is an excellent place to watch the killer whales called orcas swimming in pods, or large groups. The Haro Strait separates San Juan Island from Vancouver Island.

The lighthouse at Lime Kiln Point

Forests from the Beginning of Time

Botanist and writer Donald Culross Peattie, seeing the Olympic forests for the first time in 1940, wrote in *Audubon* magazine: "The Olympic forests are what you imagined virgin forests were when you were a child. They are tall as trees of a fairy tale, and dense as that. They are set deep, deep in ancient moss, damp, feathery sphagnum that looks as if it went back to the beginning of time." Before Peattie died, those forests he described so enthusiastically had largely been cut down. ■

The Columbia River

The second-largest river in the United States by volume of water is the Columbia. A product of the last ice age, it was formed 10,000 to 12,000 years ago. The Columbia River rises in the glaciers of Canada and travels across the border to make a huge S-shaped curve from north to south in Washington. It travels 1,214 miles (1,953 km). The largest of its many tributaries is the Snake River.

The Columbia's meandering path southward is mostly far below the level of the land. Its steep banks and cliffs make it a distant image instead of a friendly neighborhood river. The river drops 1,300 feet (397 m) in less than 900 miles (1,448 km).

A wharf along the Columbia River

The Columbia River that Lewis and Clark found was a rough, roaring river filled with rapids. These rapids kept the river from becoming a commercial highway, so the land around it was mostly useless for agriculture.

Today, the mighty river has been tamed by dams—in fact, overtamed. Historian Donald Worster has called the Columbia, with its eleven major dams and several hundred minor dams, the river that died and was reborn as money.

Rivers, Lakes, and More Dams

The walls of the Grand Coulee in central Washington stand 800 to 1,000 feet (244 to 305 m) above the old riverbed carved out by the glacial retreat thousands of years ago. This coulee is about 52 miles (84 km) long. Moses Coulee, at Moses Lake, is about the same length.

Eastern Washington was mostly desert until the Grand Coulee Dam was built in the 1930s. The dam itself is almost 1 mile (1.6 km) long. Franklin D. Roosevelt Lake—which is really a vastly widened Columbia River—stretches from the dam for a distance of 150 miles (241 km). The Grand Coulee Dam is the largest concrete structure in the United States. It stands 550 feet (168 m) tall, with the slopes of the coulee rising on each side of it.

The dam's twenty-four generators produce 6.5 million kilowatts of electricity, making it the largest single source of power in the Northwest and one of the largest in the world. Its electricity is carried throughout the West—and all the way to Chicago!

Water is piped into nearby Banks Lake, from which it is sent through pipes to irrigate about 500,000 acres (202,500 ha) of farmland. At the southern end of long Banks Lake is Dry Falls, a 3-mile (5-km)-long spectacular cliff that was once the planet's greatest waterfall.

Southeastern Washington and the bordering parts of Idaho and Oregon are called the Palouse region, after the river running through the area. The Palouse River is a tributary of the Snake. The region has its own characteristics because it lies between the west-ern Rockies and the start of the Columbia River valley. Before the coming of Europeans, it was prairie and wetland on rolling hills. The name Palouse came from the French word *pelouse,* meaning "lawn." Almost all of the original grass-lands are now farm and subur-ban areas.

Hells Canyon, near Clark-ston, is the deepest river canyon in the nation. It is almost 8,000 feet (2,440 m) from the top of the cliff above the Snake River to the bottom of the river that separates Washington from Idaho. The water at the bottom of the canyon provides a rough ride for white-water rafting and kayaking.

The Snake River running through Hells Canyon

The Fish Wheels

Until recent times, one of the most efficient and deadly ways to catch salmon was the use of a fish wheel. This was a huge water-wheel with scoops for blades. Turned by the power of the water, it scooped up massive quantities of salmon. Such wheels lined the Columbia River until environmentalists succeeded in getting the destructive wheels outlawed. ■

The Salmon Problem

The king of the Northwest has always been the salmon. There are five species of Pacific salmon—sockeye, Chinook, coho, chum, and pink. The Chinook, or king, salmon may reach 5 feet (1.5 m) in length and weigh up to 60 pounds (27 kilograms).

All salmon are hatched in freshwater, swim to the oceans, and return eventually to the freshwater of their origins to spawn, or lay eggs. The Atlantic salmon then return to the sea for more long months of feeding before returning to the rivers again. But the Pacific salmon spend two to five years at sea and return to their rivers, sometimes by leaping spectacularly up waterfalls and rapids. Then they lay their eggs and die. The eggs develop into wriggling larvae, which gradually turn into tiny fish, or fingerlings. By some amazing instinct, the fingerlings make their way to the ocean.

That's the way it's supposed to work. But when the rivers are dammed, most adult salmon cannot reach their spawning grounds. And the fingerlings of those that succeed in spawning cannot reach the sea because the giant turbines that produce electricity suck them in. The calmness of the tamed river also affects them. They need cold, rushing water to carry them out to sea.

In recent years, several species of salmon have been added to the endangered species list, and the fish catches—for both Native Americans and commercial fishing businesses—have decreased. Some of the endangered species are found in the waters around Seattle, where fishing hobbyists have been angling for years. But the growth of the city itself has destroyed the waters where these fish live and breed.

To help protect the fish, so-called fish ladders have been added to the dams. Unfortunately, many salmon climbing the ladders die from what is called supersaturation. The foaming water takes in more nitrogen from the air than the fish can stand.

To help the fingerlings reach the sea, a program was started to keep the turbines from becoming clogged with dead fish. In one of the most complex operations, workers scoop huge quantities of fingerlings into tanks on barges, transport them around the dams, and release them into the water on the other side.

Many people have tried to have the dams removed from the Columbia and Snake Rivers. But this would harm agriculture and electricity generation. The governments of the northwestern states and the U.S. government are trying to find solutions, but it may be too late for the salmon.

A purple shore crab at Olympic National Park

Wildlife

Washington has an incredible variety of wildlife. It changes character as one goes from the seashore to the tops of mountain peaks. Steelhead, shad, smelt, and several kinds of trout all live in Washington's rivers. A particularly large species of octopus is found in Puget Sound.

Many kinds of shore wildlife, including crabs, live in Puget Sound and the beaches of the Pacific. The coastal section of Olympic National Park has tide pools, where it is easy to see the spectacular creatures of the ocean. Several kinds of clams can be found in the sand including the geoduck, which runs a siphon up 3 feet (1 m) through the sand.

One of the great joys of western Washington is seeing a whale from the shore or a boat. Enthusiasts can sometimes see gray whales and orcas, or killer whales, as well as porpoises.

Small harbor seals live throughout the San Juan Islands and Puget Sound. If they come out of the water onto land, they must be left alone. The larger sea lions are more rare, but people sometimes see them in Puget Sound, too.

Roosevelt elk live in the Olympic Mountains and some back-wood sections of western Washington. Rocky Mountain elk are found in the Blue Mountains. Black-tailed deer inhabit the western part of the state, and white-tailed deer live in the northeast. Mule

A harbor seal pup at low tide

deer can be found from the slopes of the Cascades throughout most of the eastern part of the state. Canada's Selkirk Mountains, which extend a little way into northeastern Washington, are home to some rare woodland caribou.

Other mammals in Washington include cougars, coyotes, and red foxes—which aren't always red! Flying squirrels can sometimes be seen gliding from tree to tree, even in the city of Seattle.

Many black-tailed deer live in Washington.

Because a glacier separated the Cascade Mountains from the Olympic Mountains during the ice age, some of the wildlife that dominates one is not found in the other at all. The Cascades, for example, have grizzly bears, while only black bears are found in the Olympics.

One species of rattlesnake is the only poisonous reptile in Washington. It is found in the dry parts of eastern Washington. Many bald eagles nest in trees in the western part. Owls are plentiful, thanks to the protection of the northern spotted owl. Grays Harbor is a welcome place for shorebirds. Enthusiastic bird-watchers go there to see the millions of birds that find food in the tidal mudflats of the estuary off Aberdeen.

Shorebirds at Grays Harbor

Washington's Climate

Washington is kept fairly warm by ocean currents and over-ocean, or maritime, air masses. These air masses tend to drop frequent rain on the west and lose their moisture as they cross the Cascades. Olympic National Forest gets about 160 inches (406 centimeters) of precipitation each year, the highest rainfall in the lower forty-eight states. Just over the mountains, in what is called the "rain shadow," parts of eastern Washington get as little as 6 inches (15 cm) annually.

The rain-shadow effect is not limited to eastern Washington. Despite being surrounded by water, the climate of the San Juan Islands is quite dry. They are in the rain shadow formed by the Olympic Mountains.

Puget Sound's maritime climate provides cool winters and mild, pleasant summers. The average low temperature in winter is 36° Fahrenheit (2° Celsius) and the average high in summer is 69°F (21°C). The average annual rainfall is only 39 inches (99 cm), but it falls lightly about every two days out of three. Sometimes in winter, Washington's cities have major snowfalls, but the snow doesn't last long.

A Spectacular Snowfall

Mount Baker, east of Bellingham, is 10,778 feet (3,287 m) high. Between July 1998 and June 1999, 95 feet (29 m) of snow fell at the Mount Baker Ski Area. It set a record for the most snow in a year in the United States—and probably in the world. It was more than twice the average winter snowfall for Mount Baker. In June 1999, the snow pack was 18 feet (5.5 m) deep at the ski area. ■

CHAPTER SIX

A State with Everything

W hen people think of Washington, they generally think of the water world of Puget Sound, with Seattle at its center. Most of the biggest cities are on the sound, or on an inlet of the sound, making what some people have called "Pugetopolis." The major cities of Bellingham and Everett lie to the north, and Tacoma and Olympia lie to the south.

The city of Seattle with Mount Rainier in the background

Puget Sound—The Water World

Bellingham, the first small city south of the border on Puget Sound, is a beautiful old city formed out of smaller towns that flourished during the Klondike gold rush. Today, this wonderful port is the final destination of the Alaska Marine Highway. This is not a road at all, but the ferry system to the San Juans, Victoria Island, and southern Alaska. Squalicum Harbor is the second-largest harbor on Puget Sound, housing hundreds of craft, as well as whale-watch cruises.

The city of Anacortes is located on Fidalgo Island. A small, almost unnoticeable channel separates it from the mainland. Anacortes, once a major salmon-fishing port, is now the gateway to the San Juan Islands.

Opposite: Boats anchored near the San Juan Islands

The Peace Arch

Marking the western end of the long border between Canada and the United States is the large, white marble Peace Arch. Built in 1921, it was paid for by contributions from schoolchildren in both countries and constructed by volunteers. It stands with one foot in White Rock, British Columbia, and the other in Blaine, Washington. On the Canadian side of the arch the words "Brothers Dwelling Together in Unity" are engraved. On the Washington side is the inscription "Children of a Common Mother." ■

South of Anacortes is Whidbey Island. Since 1985, it has been heralded as the longest island in the lower forty-eight states. It was not that the 45-mile (72-km) island grew. It was that the U.S. Supreme Court declared Long Island in New York a peninsula! Lately, Whidbey Island has become a commuter haven for many employees of Boeing, in Everett.

The highway from Anacortes to Whidbey crosses Deception

Pass, the channel between the two islands. It got its name when Captain Vancouver was deceived into thinking it was a calm waterway. Deception Pass State Park is located on both sides of the channel.

The San Juan Islands

Ferries go to the three largest of the San Juan Islands—San Juan, Orcas, and Lopez—as well as little Shaw Island, which lies between the other three. The ferry dock on Shaw is run by the nuns who live in a convent there.

The largest of the San Juans is San Juan Island. The main village is Friday Harbor, at which all ferries stop. The island boasts San Juan Island National Historical Park and a whale museum.

Bellingham is located along Puget Sound.

The Pig War Park

In 1859, an American settler on San Juan Island killed an annoying pig that belonged to the Hudson's Bay Company. When he refused to pay for it, the Canadians insisted he be taken to court. The American settlers called for military protection, and the Canadians did likewise. Suddenly, war- ships with heavy cannon lined up against one another. No shots were fired, but the two sides established semipermanent military bases on the island. American Camp at the south end of the island and English Camp at the north now make up San Juan Island National Historical Park. ■

Orcas Island is the hilliest of the San Juans. One mountain, Mount Constitution, rises to 2,409 feet (735 m). A watchtower stands on top of it. The International Order of Odd Fellows, a fraternal organization, was founded on Orcas Island.

Lopez Island has gentler hills and is great for cycling. Several other islands are marine state parks.

Seattle—The Emerald City

Seattle was originally called Duwamps. It is probably fortunate that its name was changed to Seattle, after Chief Sealth. Some early developers called it "New York, Al-ki," which meant "New York, Bye and Bye," to the Chinooks. They hoped to see it eventually challenge New York City on the East Coast.

Seattle almost didn't survive. The Northern Pacific Railroad,

The famous Space Needle at the heart of Seattle's skyline

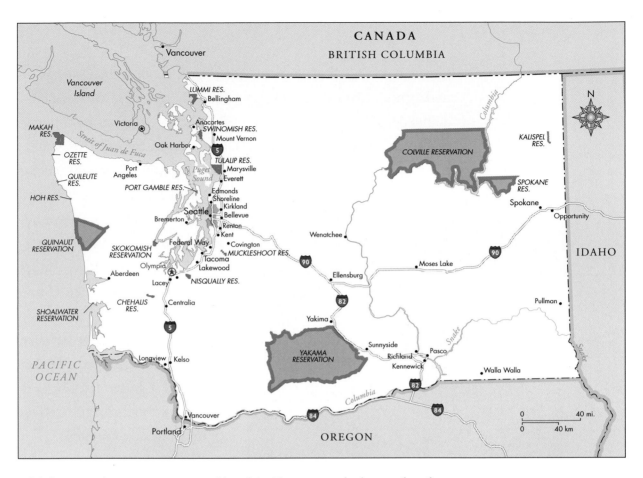

CANADA
BRITISH COLUMBIA

Washington's cities
and interstates

which owned vast amounts of land in Tacoma, tried very hard to make sure that growth on Puget Sound took place in Tacoma. Determined Seattleites got together and built their own railroad connection.

On June 6, 1889, months before Washington became a state, a large part of Seattle burned down in a fire that started in a glue pot at a furniture-maker's shop. The Great Seattle Fire gave Seattleites a chance to rebuild their city with more flair—and greater safety.

Since they were rebuilding anyway, the residents of Seattle chose to build at a higher level. To prevent floods from tidal action in Puget Sound, they raised the streets of the town between 8 and 35 feet

(2.4 and 11 m). The original streets and shops were used as an underground world for several years. Then structures were condemned and left to rot, but since 1965, intrepid tourists have joined go-at-your-own-risk tours through the underground world of Seattle.

Seattle is a long, stretched-out city between two spectacular bodies of water, Puget Sound on the west and Lake Washington on the east. Lake Washington is connected to Puget Sound by narrow Lake Union and the Lake Washington Ship Canal. Boats can move between them by going up or down in Hiram M. Chittenden Locks in Ballard. A boat can rise 26 feet (8 m) in fifteen minutes.

Seattle's waterways make getting around complicated. However, the city has a 1.3-mile (2.1-km)-long Metro Transit Tunnel that includes three bus terminals. Also, a light rail system from Everett to Tacoma is planned.

Seattle Center is a 74-acre (30-ha) area near the waterfront that houses many artistic and musical activities. The 1962

Lake Union and Seattle Center

world's fair took place here. The Space Needle, built to reflect the future in space, has remained one of the highlights of Seattle. The Pacific Science Center was the U.S. Science Pavilion at the fair. It consists of six buildings flanked by five 110-foot (33.5-m)-tall arches that are visible from long distances away.

The Monorail built for the fair still carries people 1.2 miles (2 km) from Seattle Center to Westlake Center, a shopping area. A major expansion of the Monorail is being considered for the future. A waterfront trolley runs on tracks from Pier 70 to the International District, where many people from the Far East live.

Pike Place Market is the oldest continuous farmers' market in the United States. It has been selling local produce since 1907. It was in danger of being demolished in the 1960s, but Seattleites fought to make it a historic district.

Shopping at Pike Place Market

Seattle's Pioneer Square was originally an island. The water around it was filled in. The Pioneer Building in Pioneer Square was constructed immediately after the Great Seattle Fire. Waterfall Garden Park was donated to honor the people who started the United Parcel Service (UPS). It features a 22-foot (6.7-m) waterfall. A wonderful wrought-iron, glass-topped pergola stands next to a Native American totem pole.

Klondike Gold Rush National Historical Park actually has two parts—one in Seattle and one in Skagway, Alaska. The Seattle section consists of one room in an old store located in Pioneer Park.

Seafair

Seattle's annual Seafair is a large celebration that lasts several weeks. Originally called the Potlatch, it was held on and off from 1911 to 1950. Then it became the Seafair.

It offers everything from clowns and pirates in the streets to boat races on Lake Washington to jazz concerts and parades large and small. A big Indian powwow is held in conjunction with Seafair. ■

It symbolizes the role Seattle played in the development of Alaska during the Klondike gold rush.

In the area called Fremont—which lives up to its motto "Freedom to be Peculiar"—the underpass of the Aurora Bridge features a huge troll eating a real Volkswagen. Nearby is a popular piece of public art—Richard Beyer's life-size statue, *Waiting for the Interurban*. People often think they have really come upon a train station.

Around Seattle

Many islands around Seattle were once home to people who fished for a living. Many houses were little cottages built for weekend use.

Since the coming of the computer age, however, these islands, especially Mercer Island, have become home to young people who worked at Microsoft. Many of them owned stock in Microsoft and other computer companies and became multimillionaires. The small cottages were swept away and huge houses, sometimes called megahomes, have replaced them, changing the character of the islands.

Redmond, where Microsoft is located, is across Lake Washington from Seattle. Microsoft has a campus of more than forty buildings on 300 acres (122 ha) of forested

Microsoft's headquarters is located in Redmond.

A park in downtown Bellevue

land. The campus has soccer fields and several cafeterias. More than 14,000 employees work at Microsoft.

Boeing Field takes up much of the area south of Seattle. The building in which William E. Boeing first started making airplanes in 1916 is called the Red Barn. It is now the centerpiece of the spectacular Museum of Flight.

Bellevue, a desirable place to live, stands opposite Seattle on the east side of Lake Washington. People from Bellevue and other towns reach Seattle on the longest floating bridges in the world. Evergreen Point Floating Bridge crosses the entrance to Lake Union and Mercer Island Floating Bridge carries I-90 from Mercer Island in Lake Washington into the city of Seattle.

Amazingly, just a few miles east of Bellevue in the Seattle metropolitan area is Snoqualmie Falls. At 270 feet (82 m) high, it is 100 feet (31 m) higher than Niagara Falls. The TV series *Twin Peaks* and *Northern Exposure* were filmed near here.

Tacoma Region

Sea-Tac International Airport is located between Seattle and Tacoma. An airport bus called the Hustlebus takes passengers to downtown Seattle.

Tacoma, which is the Indian name for Mount Rainier, is the

The Tacoma waterfront
on Puget Sound

third-largest city in Washington. The Northern Pacific Railroad chose this city for its terminal. Tacoma boomed after Weyerhaeuser, a huge logging company, came to town. Weyerhaeuser's world headquarters are in nearby Federal Way. Today, paper mills employ many of the city's residents. The Point Defiance Zoo and Aquarium is a world-class zoo. They have several breeding programs to rebuild endangered species.

Watching a Bridge Collapse

Tacoma Narrows Bridge connects Tacoma to the Olympic Peninsula. Only a few months after this bridge opened to traffic in 1940, winds started twisting the bridge. As crowds gathered and watched, "Galloping Gertie" collapsed on November 7, 1940. The destruction was recorded on film—which can be seen on the Internet! After the bridge's collapse, engineers tested all designs to make sure that they can withstand aerodynamic forces. The new bridge has operated safely since its opening in 1951. ■

The Capital

Olympia is Washington's state capital and a friendly small town. In 1846, two very different men—Edmund Sylvester, a fisherman, and Levi Lathrop Smith, a divinity student—got land grants next to each other. They agreed that whoever survived the other would own both pieces of land. Smith died in an overturned canoe, and Sylvestor owned the town called Smithfield. In 1851, Congress placed a customs house there, the first one on Puget Sound. A resident succeeded in changing the name Smithfield to Olympia.

Within months, the town had stores, a church, and even a newspaper. In November 1853, Isaac I. Stevens arrived as the new territory's governor. He named the thriving town the territorial capital. Edmund Sylvester donated land for the new capitol.

The first territorial legislature met above a store in Olympia on February 27, 1854. From 1863 to 1903, the legislature met in a temporary building. The grounds in front of the Old State Capitol are Sylvester Park. The narrow and beautifully landscaped Capitol Lake lies in front of the various state buildings.

Walking along Broadway Avenue, leading to the capitol, pedestrians can take a moment to enjoy a lighthearted dance step. In eight places along the avenue, bronze footprints are embedded in the sidewalks in the diagram of dance steps.

Western Washington

The Olympic Peninsula is the part of Washington north of Grays Harbor between Puget Sound and the ocean. The core of the peninsula as well as a strip along the coast make up Olympia National Park. It includes the only temperate rain forest in the United States.

Loggers worked on the rest of the peninsula, and the forests show signs that they were once cut. The large Quinault Indian Reservation and two smaller reservations—Makah and Ozette—take up most of the remainder of the peninsula.

The towns of Port Angeles, Port Townsend, and Sequim lie at the top of the peninsula on the Strait of Juan de Fuca. Port Angeles, the largest town on the peninsula, hosts several million visitors to the national park each year.

Kitsap is a peninsula off the Olympic Peninsula—or it would be if a canal didn't separate the two. It lies across Puget Sound from Seattle and appears to have more water than land. The city of Bremerton lies at its southern end, almost hidden behind ships stored by the U.S. Navy. Bainbridge Island lies off Bremerton.

Aberdeen and Hoquiam are twin cities on the eastern tip of Grays Harbor. Three different rivers run into the harbor, so there is plenty of waterfront living here. The towns got started because those rivers were used for moving logs from the forests to the sawmills. Grays Harbor National Wildlife Refuge lies west of Hoquiam.

Almost at the mouth of the Columbia River—and the southwestern corner of the state—is Willapa Bay. The shoreline is a long strip of land called Long Beach. It is probably the longest beach in

Port Angeles lies on the Strait of Juan de Fuca.

the world. A wide strip of sand goes around the whole 28-mile (45-km) edge of the peninsula. This area is especially popular with kite fliers, who can run freely along the shore. The World Kite Museum and Hall of Fame is located in the town of Long Beach.

The Washington State International Kite Festival at Long Beach

Along the Columbia

Many of Washington's earliest towns and villages started along the Columbia River. First the Lewis and Clark Expedition and then many settlers came into the territory on the river. A fur trader who didn't know he had found a river named the southernmost tip of the coast at the mouth of the river Cape Disappointment.

The twin towns of Longview and Kelso are located where the Cowlitz River joins the Columbia, which turns southward. The earliest settlers met here to create a petition to Congress to form a separate territory on the northern side of the river. They got their wish.

For Europeans, the Northwest began in Vancouver, across from Portland, Oregon. Vancouver, the oldest non–Native American community in the region, is usually referred to as Vancouver, USA, to avoid confusion with Vancouver, in British Columbia, Canada. On the edge of downtown Vancouver, USA, is Fort Vancouver National Historic Site, a rebuilt Hudson's Bay Company post.

Washougal is Washington's southernmost point, where the Columbia River briefly dips southward. It is considered the entrance to the spectacular Columbia River Gorge. In places, the beautiful gorge is so narrow that settlers arriving in covered wagons had to take their wagons apart and float them down the river.

Maryhill Museum

Near the eastern end of the gorge is Maryhill, named by its founder, Sam Hill, for his women relatives. He planned to start a Quaker community here, but his wife left him and he abandoned a half-completed mansion. After World War I, famed dancer Loie Fuller persuaded Hill to finish the mansion as a museum. It now houses an amazing collection of beautiful and strange historic items, including a large collection of sculptures by artist Auguste Rodin. Also on the property is a concrete copy of Stonehenge, the mysterious and ancient circle of standing stones in southern England.

Just after McNary Dam, the river turns north and no longer forms the border with Oregon. This is called the Tri-Cities area for the three large—and growing—towns of Richland, Kennewick, and Pasco.

The town of Richland did not even exist until the DuPont Company built the town for 3,275 families of DuPont workers. Residents of the area were moved out to make room for these newcomers. Richland has often been called Atomic City because the Hanford Atomic Works helped to develop the atomic bomb there in the 1940s.

The Endangered Hanford Reach

A 51-mile (82-km) stretch of the Columbia upstream from Richland called Hanford Reach has been named the most endangered river in America by American Rivers, a conservation organization. It is not because of nearby radioactivity but because the river is now open to develop- ment. Hanford Reach was isolated for so long that it is the least spoiled part of the Columbia. It is also the last spawning ground of the Chinook salmon on the big river. Many people are working to have the reach declared a Wild and Scenic River, which would protect it from human activity. ■

The Tri-Cities area developed along with the Hanford reservation, which occupies most of the area north of it. The Snake River, the Columbia's main tributary, joins the Columbia at Kennewick.

Central Washington

East of the Cascades in several fertile valleys are a number of large towns. The Yakima Valley stretches westward from the Columbia River. Irrigation in Washington began here. The city of Yakima lies at the northeastern tip of the large Yakama Indian Reservation.

Kennewick Man

More than 9,300 years ago, a hunter was buried on the banks of the Columbia River near Kennewick in eastern Washington. Students hiking beside the river found the remains of the well-preserved human in 1996. National Park Service archaeologists say tests show he was a Native American, and, in 2000, his bones were returned to the tribes now located in Washington. Kennewick Man was about 5 feet 9 inches (175 cm) tall. He had lived most of his life with a spear point in his hip and died when he was about forty years old. ■

North of Yakima, also in the valley, is Ellensburg. As a reminder that Washington is part of the West, Ellensburg is home to the famed Ellensburg Rodeo, which takes place every Labor Day weekend. Central Washington University is also in Ellensburg.

Still farther north in the heart of the state is *Cle Elum*, which means "swift water" in the Kittitas Indian language. Originally a gold claim and then a coal-mining town, today it is the gateway to two national forests, the Wenatchee and the Mount Baker-Snoqualmie.

On the Columbia River itself is Wenatchee, the focal point of four fruit-growing valleys—Okanogan, Entiat, Lake Chelan, and Methow. In the north-central part of the state, mining was once an important activity, but few mines produced for long. Now there are ghost towns in the region, though many of them have disappeared into the greenery of Okanogan National Forest.

Ellensburg is known for its annual rodeo.

An Alpine Village

The town of Leavenworth near Wenatchee was left behind by the railroads and business in the 1960s. The town decided to become something else—an Alpine village in the Northwest. The whole town was redone with a Swiss look and all new construction. The town succeeded in turning around its fortunes. ■

North of Wenatchee is the town of Chelan, the geographic center of the state. Starting at the town and stretching 55 miles (88 km) into the rugged Cascades is Lake Chelan. It is as narrow as a river in many places, but it is the third-deepest lake in the nation—1,489 feet (454 m) deep. The lake bed is 400 feet (122 m) below sea level.

The Grand Coulee Dam stands where the Columbia River enters the 55-mile (89-km)-long gorge called the Grand Coulee. The dam, built during the Great Depression and used for irrigation after World War II, revolutionized the area. A laser light show over the dam takes place at night during the summer months. Visitors can tour the dam during the day.

The river becomes Roosevelt Lake along the Colville Indian Reservation and Colville National Forest. They were named for Andrew Colville, governor of the Hudson's Bay Company.

The many tribes of Native Americans in the region are collectively called Colville Indians. In 1994, the government paid the Colville tribes $53 million—plus an annual payment—for having ruined their salmon fishing by building Grand Coulee Dam.

The East

Spokane is the second-largest city in Washington. The city began as Spokane Falls in 1872 when a sawmill was built at the rapids on the Spokane River. The name came from the *Spokan* Indians, which means "Sun People." Spokane grew quickly as a wheat-growing and flour-milling center. Today, it is the main city of a huge business area that covers parts of Washington, Oregon, Idaho, Montana, and British Columbia.

Spokane came into its own when the city held a world's fair in

1974. The theme for the fair was "Celebrating Man's Fresh New Environment." The site was an island in the middle of the Spokane River. When the waterfront was cleaned up for the fair, the spectacular Spokane Falls became visible from the city center. In Riverfront Park, a giant red Radio Flyer wagon stands with a slide for its handle.

Clarkston, in the far southeastern corner of the state, lies just across the Snake River from Lewiston, Idaho. Although Clarkston is 450 miles (724 km) from the sea, it is a seaport. Container ships travel up the Columbia and Snake Rivers to drop off and pick up cargo.

Walla Walla means "many rapid rivers." This beautiful city is one of the oldest in Washington. Whitman Mission National Historical Monument is located nearby. Territorial Governor Stevens once held an Indian council here. It was only a small town when rumors of gold brought many prospectors through on their way north, leaving the town—if not the prospectors—more prosperous.

Spokane's Riverfront Park

The popular toy building logs called Lincoln Logs are made in Walla Walla. John Lloyd Wright, son of famed Chicago architect Frank Lloyd Wright, invented these toys in 1920.

East of Walla Walla are the Blue Mountains, one of the wagon trains' great challenges. After the settlers got through safely, they were on their way to becoming Washingtonians.

CHAPTER SEVEN

Cascade Government

Inside the capitol dome

W hen Washington was about to be admitted as a state, a committee set about designing the state seal. The design was filled with figures logging and farming, carrying out the businesses of the state. There is an interesting legend about what happened next. A jeweler named Charles Talcott, after seeing the committee's design, pulled out a postage stamp bearing the likeness of President George Washington and stuck it down on the design, proclaiming it the state seal. This simple commemoration of the nation's first president has been the state seal ever since.

Washington's state flag was adopted on March 5, 1923. It shows the seal mounted on a dark green background that represents the state's magnificent forests.

Washington had no official state capital on the day it became a state. When the territory-wide election was held, no city won a majority of the votes, so the state entered the Union without a capital. Olympia was chosen by a wide margin in the next balloting.

The Executive Branch

The state's chief executive officer is the governor. Then comes the lieutenant governor and the secretary of state. The governor has the power to veto, or refuse to sign, all kinds of legislation. Six other of the top nine officials of the state's executive branch are also

Opposite: The capitol in Olympia

elected. This system allows for a wider distribution of power than exists in states with only a governor and lieutenant governor.

Two financial positions are treasurer and auditor. The attorney general heads the legal system. The commissioner of public lands supervises the Department of Natural Resources. The insurance commissioner is responsible for consumer protection. The superintendent of public instruction manages the state's educational system. To keep politics out of education, candidates for this position do not run as members of a political party.

One of the most unusual agencies within the executive branch is the Salmon Recovery Office. It exists to protect fifteen threatened or endangered salmon species and subspecies. This problem affects almost every county in the state. It has a huge effect on the state's Native Americans, too. This office works with biologists, environmentalists, and the U.S. government to bring salmon back to Washington waters.

Washington's Governors

Name	Party	Term	Name	Party	Term
Elisha P. Ferry	Rep.	1889–1893	Arthur B. Langlie	Rep.	1941–1945
John McGraw	Rep.	1893–1897	Monrad C. Wallgren	Dem.	1945–1949
John Rogers	Dem.-Pop.	1897–1901	Arthur B. Langlie	Rep.	1949–1957
Henry McBride	Rep.	1901–1905	Albert D. Rosellini	Dem.	1957–1965
Albert E. Mead	Rep.	1905–1909	Daniel J. Evans	Rep.	1965–1977
Samuel G. Cosgrove	Rep.	1909	Dixy Lee Ray	Dem.	1977–1981
Marion E. Hay	Rep.	1909–1913	John D. Spellman	Rep.	1981–1985
Ernest Lister	Dem.	1913–1919	Booth Gardner	Dem.	1985–1993
Louis F. Hart	Rep.	1919–1925	Mike Lowry	Dem.	1993–1997
Roland H. Hartley	Rep.	1925–1933	Gary Locke	Dem.	1997–
Clarence D. Martin	Dem.	1933–1941			

A Woman Governor

Dixy Lee Ray, born in Tacoma, was a biologist who headed the Pacific Science Center in Seattle. She was known throughout the country for her televised lectures on various science subjects. In 1972, President Richard Nixon appointed Ray to head the U.S. Atomic Energy Commission. Four years later, she returned to Washington to run for governor against Republican John Spellman. When she won, she became Washington's first woman governor as well as the first U.S. governor to have a doctorate. She served only one term. ■

The Legislature

Each of the forty-nine districts in the state sends one senator and two representatives to the state legislature in Olympia. The representatives are elected for two-year terms and the senators for four-year terms. Washington sends nine people to the U.S. House of Representatives and two to the U.S. Senate.

An African-American named George Washington Bush was one of the earliest settlers to arrive in the Puget Sound area, south of Olympia. Apparently he and his wife had been servants of a family named Stevenson. Eventually, the Bush couple inherited money from the Stevenson family and moved west. Bush settled at Bush Prairie, which became part of Tumwater. Their son, named George, was elected to the first state legislature in 1889.

The constitution revision of 1909 gave women the right to vote in state and local elections and serve on juries. It also opened up the legislature to women. In 1912, two women were elected to the legislature. In 1999, about 40 percent of Washington legislators were women, one of the highest percentages among the states.

Like many other states, Washington is divided politically. Voters in the eastern, farming part of the state are mostly Republican. Voters in the western, urban part of the state are mostly Democrat.

A Chinese-American Governor

In 1997, Gary Locke became the nation's first Chinese-American governor. Born in Seattle in 1950, Locke attended Yale University and earned a law degree from Boston University. He was elected to the state house of representatives in 1982. As governor of Washington, Locke has emphasized improving education in the state. ■

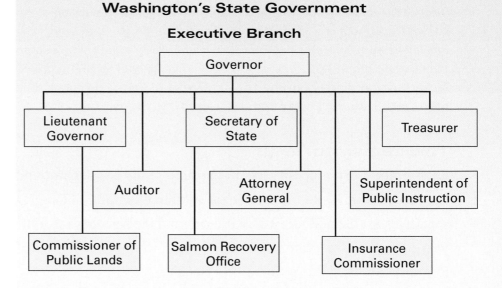

Washington's State Government

Executive Branch

- Governor
  - Lieutenant Governor
    - Commissioner of Public Lands
  - Auditor
  - Secretary of State
    - Salmon Recovery Office
  - Attorney General
  - Superintendent of Public Instruction
    - Insurance Commissioner
  - Treasurer

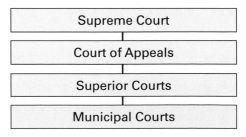

Legislative Branch

- Senate
- House of Representatives

Judicial Branch

- Supreme Court
- Court of Appeals
- Superior Courts
- Municipal Courts

The Courts

The same forty-nine districts that elect representatives to the state legislature are also court districts. Municipal courts in each district hear criminal and civil cases. These cases can go to the twenty-nine superior courts. The superior courts are the main courts where jury trials take place.

The state constitution originally called for five justices to serve on the state supreme court. Today that number has risen to nine. In 1969, the state's court of appeals was founded. Since then, fewer cases have reached the supreme court. The court of appeals functions through three divisions, with a total of nineteen judges. The state supreme court meets in the Temple of Justice, which is the oldest building on the capitol campus in Olympia. It has been used since 1913 and was recently modified.

The courthouse in Columbia County

Do I Vote or Don't I?

In 1883, the territorial legislature gave Washington women the right to vote in its elections. However, the federal courts quickly ruled the move unconstitutional. In 1888, the determined legislature voted again to give women the vote. Again, it was declared unconstitutional. The following year, the public voted for a state constitution that was approved for statehood. The right of women to vote was left out. In 1909, the state legislature again approved woman suffrage. The following year, voters approved it as the fifth amendment to the state constitution. ■

Justice Douglas

William O. Douglas grew up in Yakima, walking the hills and growing to love the outdoors. After teaching school in Yakima for a brief period, he gave up life in the outdoors to become a lawyer. He already had a reputation as a legal scholar when President Franklin D. Roosevelt appointed him to the newly created Securities and Exchange Commission (SEC) and then to the U.S. Supreme Court. Douglas served on the court from 1939 to 1975. It was the longest tenure of any justice. He became as well known for his books on nature and the environment as for his judicial opinions. ■

The state has thirty-nine counties. The largest county by area is Okanogan; the smallest is San Juan. The largest by population is King County, which contains Seattle. The smallest is Garfield County in the Palouse.

Washington has no state income tax. Such a tax is prohibited by the state's constitution. The state depends, therefore, on sales taxes. In 1999, the citizens voted to require that the people approve any tax increase.

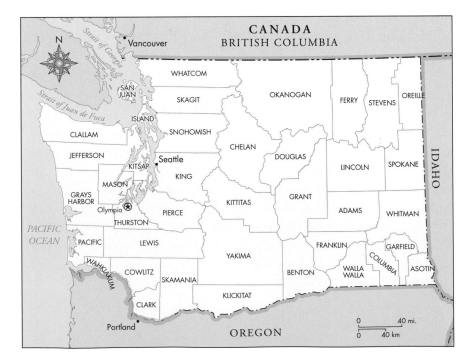

Washington's counties

Washington's State Flag and Seal

The first Washington state flag was adopted in 1923. It is the state seal on a green background. The green field stands for the state's many forests.

The first Washington state seal was adopted in 1889. The state seal has a picture of George Washington with the words THE SEAL OF THE STATE OF WASHINGTON and the year 1889 around it. In 1967, the state legislature readopted the state flag and seal with a portrait of George Washington by American painter Gilbert Stuart. ■

Washington's State Song
"Washington, My Home"

This was chosen the state song in 1959 only hours after writer Helen Davis and arranger Stuart Churchill first performed it for the legislature.

Our verdant forest green,
Caressed by silv'ry stream.
From mountain peak
to fields of wheat,
Washington, my home.
There's peace you feel and
understand.
In this, our own beloved land.

We greet the day with head
held high,
And forward ever is our cry.

We'll happy ever be
As people always free.
For you and me a destiny;
Washington my home.
For you and me a destiny;

Washington my home.

(Chorus)
Washington, my home;
Wherever I may roam;
This is my land, my native
land,
Washington, my home.

Washington's State Symbols

State flower: Coast, or western, rhododendron (left) In 1892, Washington women selected this flower as the state's official flower to enter an exhibit at the 1893 World's Columbian Exposition in Chicago. Rhododendrons are moisture-loving evergreen shrubs with clusters of flowers in various shades of pink, red, and purple.

State bird: Willow goldfinch or wild canary A little yellow bird with black wings, the goldfinch was the second state bird. Schoolchildren chose the first state bird, the meadowlark, in 1928. Already the official bird of seven other states, the meadowlark was replaced by the goldfinch in 1951, when the state's schoolchildren—and the legislature—chose it.

State tree: Western hemlock In 1946, Washington newspapers picked the western red cedar as the state's official state tree. State Representative George Adams of Mason County pleaded with the legislature to adopt the western hemlock as "the backbone of this state's forest industry." Adams got his wish in 1947.

State fish: Steelhead trout Adopted by the legislature in 1969, the steelhead trout is immensely popular for recreational fishing. It is a variety of the rainbow trout, but unlike the rainbow, lives in the ocean, returning to freshwater rivers only to spawn.

State fruit: Apple The Washington legislature chose the state's centennial year of 1989 to name the apple the state fruit. Washington is the nation's top apple-producing state, and the apple trees of eastern Washington make up one of the largest industries in the state.

State grass: Bluebunch wheatgrass Bluebunch wheatgrass is a prairie grass in eastern Washington. Settlers appreciated this grass, which remains important to the state's agriculture. It was adopted by the legislature in 1989.

State fossil: Columbian mammoth Fossils of this species of elephant, which died out about 10,000 years ago, were found recently on the Olympic Peninsula. Students from Windsor Elementary School near Cheney led an effort to have this mammoth—the largest in the world—designated the state fossil. They succeeded in 1998.

State gem: Petrified wood Swampland trees from ancient times have been preserved as stone by the intrusion of minerals into the cells of the original wood. This beautiful stone was adopted as the state gem in 1975. It can be seen at Ginkgo Petrified Forest State Park in Vantage.

State dance: Square dance On April 17, 1979, the square dance became the official Washington state dance in recognition of the quadrille dance, a square dance that the pioneers brought with them.

State ship: *President Washington* The *President Washington,* a container ship, was the first state ship to be adopted by any state. It was adopted in 1983 as a symbol of Washington's trade with the nations across the Pacific Ocean.

State tartan: Washington state tartan A tartan is a weaving design often called "plaid." The Washington state tartan was designed in 1988 to commemorate the centennial and signed into law in 1991. The green background rep-resents the forests of Washington. The other colors are blue for the lakes, rivers, and the ocean; white for snowcapped mountains; red for apple and cherry crops; yellow for wheat and grain crops; and black for the Mount St. Helens' eruption.

State insect: Green darner dragonfly Students at Crestwood Elementary School in Kent proposed a state insect to the legislature. Then, in 1997, students from more than 100 school districts chose the common green darner dragonfly (above), also known as the mosquito hawk. This green-bodied insect has a wingspan of 4 to 6 inches (10 to 15 cm).

CHAPTER EIGHT

From Ships to Software

The Evergreen State's greatest natural resource has always been its forests. They were the natural resources that drew settlers to the region. Sawmills, and then papermills, sprang up by the hundreds.

Frederick Weyerhaeuser was a German immigrant who started a small sawmill in Illinois. He and his partners did well enough to move north into Wisconsin, where they bought timberland. He became one of

One of Washington's many sawmills

the great "lumber barons" whose loggers wiped out the old forests of the upper Midwest. At the beginning of the twentieth century, Weyerhaeuser and his partners bought up 900,000 acres (364,500 ha) of forestland in the West from the Northern Pacific Railway at a cost of only $6 per 1 acre (0.4 ha). He then built the nation's largest sawmill in Everett. Weyerhaeuser became the biggest name in timber in the Northwest.

In the 1920s, Washington became a major supplier of paper and pulp. The pulp mills used trees such as hemlock, which had been regarded as waste since they were useless for lumber. Eventually, many pulp mills merged to become the giant paper company called Crown Zellerbach.

Opposite: Crates of apples ready for shipment

The Mount St. Helens Rescue

Much of the land around Mount St. Helens was a huge tree farm owned by Weyerhaeuser. The blast of the mountain's eruption in 1980 tore down millions of trees. For two years, more than 1,000 Weyerhaeuser employees worked to salvage all the logs they could before the wood rotted. They sometimes sent 600 loaded trucks a day out of the area. Enough logs were salvaged for lumber to build 85,000 houses. In the 1980s, more than 18 million tree seedlings were planted in the volcanic ash. ■

Mining

Mineral resources played an important role in the settlement of northeastern Washington. In the days of the western gold rushes, prospectors searched everywhere for gold that they could find by sifting through gravel. They made their first strike in Washington in 1855 near the Pend Oreille River. Their success brought more prospectors, as well as the Yakama Indian War. It was another thirty years before gold mines were started that processed gold from the ore that was removed.

In the following decades, small deposits of gold, and sometimes silver, have been found throughout the eastern part of the state. They have never been large enough to affect the state's economy much, however.

What Washington Grows, Manufactures, and Mines

Agriculture	Manufacturing	Mining
Apples	Food products	Coal
Beef cattle	Machinery	Gold
Milk	Paper products	Sand and gravel
Timber	Transportation	
Wheat		

Crops and Workers

As well-irrigated farm fields replaced the prairie in the 1880s, the far eastern part of Washington became a major grain-growing area. However, areas farther west did not have the good natural irrigation of the east. Instead, crops there depended on water supplied by artificial waterways.

Grain elevators amid Washington fields

Apple orchards are profitable for central Washington.

Central Washington's orchards got their start in 1905, when the U.S. government began irrigation projects to distribute water throughout the Yakima and Okanogan Valleys. Congress had seen the lumber companies end up with vast holdings after it passed the Timber and Stone Act in 1878. This time, they decreed that only enough water to irrigate 160 acres (65 ha) would be allotted to any land-owner, no matter how much land he owned. Orchards were one of the few crops that could be profitable on such a small piece of land.

Hiram Smith planted the

Washington Apple Pie

Washington apples make this famous traditional dessert even better.

Ingredients:

    2 9-inch pie crusts
    8 cups tart apples
    1/4 cup flour
    1/3 to 2/3 cup sugar
    1/2 teaspoon nutmeg
    1/2 teaspoon cinnamon
    a dash of salt
    2 tablespoons butter

Directions:

Preheat oven to 425°F.

Place one pie crust into a 9-inch pie plate.

Peel and slice apples. In a large bowl, mix flour, sugar, nutmeg, cinnamon, and salt. Stir in apples, then pour into the pie crust. Dab with butter.

Lay top crust over the pie, and cut slits in the top. Seal the edges of the crust together.

Bake 40 to 50 minutes or until crust is golden and juice begins to bubble through the slits.

first apple trees known to have been planted in Washington, near Oroville in 1854. It was another forty years before the first railway car loaded with Washington apples left the state to deliver them to consumers around the country. Today, Washington harvests and ships more than 100 million boxes of apples annually. A museum in Wenatchee displays labels from many different companies and varieties of apples.

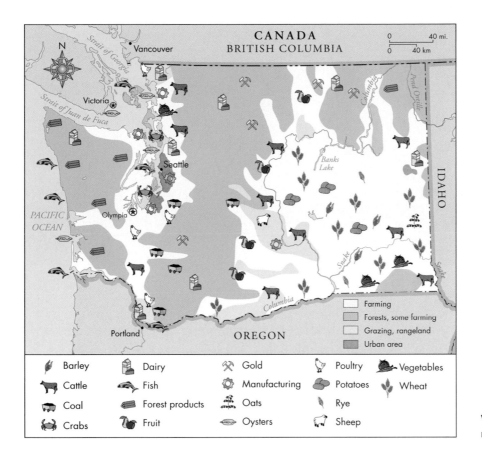

CANADA
BRITISH COLUMBIA

Vancouver

Victoria

Seattle

Olympia

PACIFIC
OCEAN

Banks
Lake

IDAHO

Portland

OREGON

Strait of Georgia

Strait of Juan de Fuca

Columbia

Snake

Columbia

Pend Oreille

Snake

0   40 mi.
0   40 km

N

	Farming
	Forests, some farming
	Grazing, rangeland
	Urban area

🌾 Barley	🏭 Dairy	⛏ Gold	🐓 Poultry	🎩 Vegetables
🐄 Cattle	🐬 Fish	⚙ Manufacturing	☁ Potatoes	🌾 Wheat
🚃 Coal	🪵 Forest products	🌱 Oats	🌿 Rye	
🦀 Crabs	🐚 Fruit	🦪 Oysters	🐑 Sheep	

Washington's natural resources

An Imported Crop from the Sea

Willapa Bay produces about 25 percent of all oysters consumed in the United States. The oysters are not native to the bay, however. Seed oysters were brought in from the East in the late 1800s. Unfortunately, an introduced grass began overwhelming parts of the bay in the 1990s. Oystermen and landowners, including the Nature Conservancy, which is usually opposed to pesticide spraying, are hoping to get permission to use a pesticide in the bay to kill the foreign grasses and save the oyster crop. ■

State Fairs

Instead of just one big state fair to celebrate agriculture, Washington has three. Yakima is the headquarters of the Central Washington State Fair. The Western Washington Fair is held in September in Puyallup (above). Washington's largest state fair is the Evergreen State Fair, held in Monroe. ■

Although Idaho is usually thought of as the "potato state," Washington has 395 growers producing more potatoes per acre than any other potato farmers in the world. In 1999, they grew more than 4.7 million tons, making potatoes the second-largest crop in the state.

About 60,000 mostly Hispanic workers harvest the state's crops. These workers did not benefit at all from the economic boom of the 1990s. In fact, many of them now live in even worse conditions. The federal government declared their camps unhealthy and did not allow them to live there anymore. Many workers and their families remain homeless.

Shipping

Bainbridge Island was the site of a shipbuilding industry in the days of the tall-masted schooners. It is still in the boat business, with the Washington State Ferry System having its ship-repair facility there. The ferries make more than 3,300 trips each week. The largest, the *Tacoma,* can carry 2,500 passengers and 200 cars.

The fleet of pleasure craft in Puget Sound is huge—the region is a paradise for boaters. But working boats are just as important. The Puget Sound region is important to commercial fishing. The Fishermen's Terminal at Ballard is the headquarters for more than 700 boats that bring in $1.5 billion worth of fish a year.

Oceangoing ships come into Puget Sound. Both the Port of Seattle and the Port of Tacoma are among the largest ports in the country to handle containers. That means that huge rectangular

Ships being loaded at the Port of Tacoma

boxes are off-loaded from ships onto the wheels of semi trucks, which then carry the containers—mostly from the Far East—throughout the United States. These containers can also be placed on railway cars.

Seattle has long been the setting-off point for adventurers and businessmen going to Alaska. Today it serves a similar purpose for tourists. Most Alaska Airlines planes land at Sea-Tac Airport, from which travelers can go in all directions. Cruise ships that take the Inner Passage to Alaska leave from Puget Sound.

The Boeing Company

The Boeing Company, the largest airplane company in the world, began business in 1916. It was built by William E. Boeing and his partner, G. Conrad Westerveldt, and housed in a wooden barracks-like building that had been a boathouse. Spruce wood from the Olympic Peninsula was valuable for building airplanes.

Following World War I, when airplanes were first used, the firm built many airplanes for carrying mail, which is how commercial aviation began in the United States. William Boeing also started an airline, United—the first airline to have flight attendants. The government forced him to split up the company and United Airlines became a separate company.

Boeing is the largest airplane builder in the world.

Today, Boeing has plants in various places throughout the world. Their headquarters in Everett is flanked by the largest structure in the world. It covers almost 100 acres (41 ha), or about 100 football fields. Employees ride bicycles to get around inside it. Oddly enough, the huge building is not heated. The machinery and the active people inside it keep warm by manufacturing 747s, 767s, and 777s.

Names Out of Washington

John Nordstrom, a Swedish immigrant, found the seed money for his future in the goldfields of the Klondike. He and a shoe-store owner named Carl Wallin started in business together in Seattle in 1901. John's sons—Everett, Elmer, and Lloyd—built the business from that one shoe store into the growing luxury-clothing store chain Nordstrom is today.

Jim Casey started the United Parcel Service (UPS) in 1907. Today, UPS is the world's largest package-delivery service. Its headquarters are now in Atlanta, Georgia.

Gray Line Tours was begun in Seattle in 1910 when visitors started coming to Seattle as a result of the Alaska-Yukon-Pacific Exposition. A young restaurant owner named Louis Bush cleaned up and decorated a Mack Truck, which he then used to offer sightseeing trips. Every major city in the country now offers Gray Line Tours.

Eddie Bauer opened an outdoor and sporting-goods store in downtown Seattle in 1920. He introduced the down-filled jacket, and during World War II, the firm produced jackets that kept pilots warm during high-altitude flight. The single store has grown into

The original Starbucks Coffee in Pike Place Market

570 shops worldwide as well as a big online store.

In 1971, three teachers from California started Starbucks Coffee. They began with a small shop in Pike Place Market. Eventually they had people the world over relishing such coffee drinks as lattes and espressos in 930 stores. The company is named for the first mate who loved coffee in the Herman Melville novel *Moby Dick.*

Wizards of the Coast, producers of Magic: The Gathering and Pokémon card games, was begun in Seattle in the early 1990s. This international company, now owned by Hasbro, also owns Dungeons & Dragons role-playing games and novels.

The Computer World of the Future

In the early 1970s, Bill Gates, a freshman at Harvard University, and his friend Paul Allen developed a workable version of the BASIC programming language for the Altair computer. This was the first "language" developed to run a computer meant for personal use instead of the big mainframes that had been in use until then. The next winter, Gates and Allen formed a partnership that they called Micro-Soft.

Soon the Commodore and the TRS-80 were on the market

The Founders of Microsoft

Bill Gates (right) was born in Seattle in 1955, the son of an attorney and a schoolteacher. Gates became fascinated by computers at the age of thirteen when his school, a private institution in Seattle called Lakeside School, got a computer teletype machine. Gates met a fellow student and electronics addict named Paul Allen. In their spare time, the two boys worked on a computer language.

Then at Harvard University, Gates lived down the hall from Steve Ballmer, who later became president of Microsoft. Gates left the university in his junior year to develop BASIC and start Microsoft with Allen. In 1999, Gates and his wife, Melinda, a former Microsoft employee, created the Bill and Melinda Gates Foundation, which funds health and reading programs around the world.

Paul Allen concentrated on computer hardware at Microsoft until 1983, when he was diagnosed with cancer. After recovering from the illness, he bought several companies, including a large cable company called Charter Communications. The third-wealthiest man in the United States, Paul Allen owns the Seattle Seahawks football team and donates money to various organizations. ■

using BASIC, and the personal computer business was off and running, with Microsoft, as it was officially named, at the helm. At the beginning of 1979, Microsoft was moved to Bellevue, Washington, and the state's business landscape began to change.

In 1980, IBM hired Microsoft to create a language and operating system for their personal computer. The result was Microsoft Disk Operating System, or MS-DOS. IBM, without much forethought, gave Microsoft the right to develop MS-DOS for other computers. As a result of that decision, MS-DOS eventually became Windows; Microsoft, the fastest-growing technology company in history; Bill Gates, the world's richest man; and the Seattle area, the headquarters of the computer revolution. Microsoft now employs about 70,000 people worldwide.

CHAPTER NINE

Washingtonians

Native Americans have a long history in Washington.

A1998 survey determined that Washington had 5,685,304 people, which was 800,000 more than in the 1990 federal census. Most of the newcomers moved into the western Puget Sound region. Thirty percent of the people live in King County (the Seattle area). Another 30 percent live in other Puget Sound communities, leaving about 2 million people to occupy the remainder of the state.

The people in the Puget Sound area tend to be younger than other Washingtonians. Many of them came to Washington to participate in the burgeoning technological economy, while taking advantage of the state's many natural attractions.

The First Washingtonians

The first Washingtonians, of course, were Native Americans. The Northwest Coast Indians lived in isolation from other tribes and developed their own culture. About 100,000 Indians lived along the coast when the Europeans arrived.

The Europeans found forty-two divisions, or tribes, of the Salish Indians. They spoke many different languages that were categorized as Coastal Salish and Interior Salish. (A few tribes in the southeastern part of the state are called Shahaptian speakers.) The two groups had little contact with each other before historic times.

During the early days of settlement, the Indian language that was used by all tribes, as well as by white fur trappers, was Chinook, spoken by a tribe in Oregon. Fur traders added English and French terms to Chinook.

Opposite: Enjoying a sunny day in Seattle

The Makah Indian reservation on the shores of Neah Bay

Today, Washington has twenty-seven reservations; only two states have more. Most of these reservations are quite small, with a total of about 81,000 individuals living on them. For example, the Sauk-Suiattle people own two plots of land totaling 23 acres (9.3 ha) in two counties. The tribe has 235 members. In all, only 1.81 percent of Washington's people are Native Americans.

The largest tribes are the Yakama (they changed the spelling of their name from Yakima in 1994) in the east and the Lummi and Quinault in the west. The Coastal Salish tribes are grouped together as Puget Sound Salish, with about 10,000 members.

The Yakama people live on the Columbia Plateau, between the Rockies and the Cascades. Their native language, Sahaptin, is also spoken by several other groups, including Nez Perce and Cayuse. The Yakama have long thrived on salmon fishing.

The Potlatch

The Salish peoples of the Northwest Coast used to perform a ceremonial giving away of gifts and even property. The ceremony was called a *potlatch,* a Chinook word meaning "to give away." The public display of generosity showed off a person's social position. Sometimes, if a person had done wrong, he and his family would hold a potlatch to get back into the tribe's good graces. Originally, a potlatch was held by a new chief to get the members of the tribe on his side or to celebrate a marriage.

Potlatches were outlawed in Canada and the United States in the early 1900s. In British Columbia, among the Kwakiutl people, they are being held again. ■

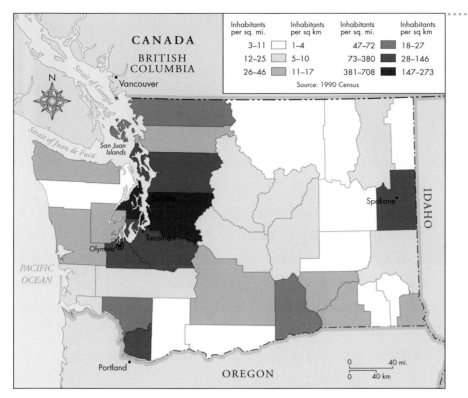

Inhabitants per sq. mi.		Inhabitants per sq km	Inhabitants per sq. mi.		Inhabitants per sq km
3–11		1–4	47–72		18–27
12–25		5–10	73–380		28–146
26–46		11–17	381–708		147–273

Source: 1990 Census

CANADA
BRITISH COLUMBIA

Strait of Georgia
Vancouver
Strait of Juan de Fuca
San Juan Islands
Seattle
Tacoma
Olympia
PACIFIC OCEAN
Spokane
IDAHO
Portland
OREGON

0   40 mi.
0   40 km

Washington's population density

Native Americans continue many traditions, including those related to salmon fishing.

A group of small related tribes who once lived along the upper Columbia River are known as the Colville Confederated Tribes. Their native language is Salish. These tribes were forced to share one reservation in 1872. Then, after only a few months, the site of that reservation was cut in half so that more settlers could acquire land in the area and prospectors could hunt for gold.

Not all Native Americans belong to officially recognized tribes. Groups seeking official recognition by the U.S. government include the Snohomish, Samish, Duwamish, and Snoqualmoo of Whidbey Island.

Building for the Future

The Native American tribes of Washington are trying to build businesses based on tourism in order to combat the high unemployment among their people. In 2000, twelve of the twenty-seven recognized tribes ran gambling casinos, though they have a difficult time competing with the casinos in places with better weather.

The Quinault Indians have a recreation area in Ocean Shores in Grays Harbor County. The Yakama people have a similar center in Toppenish. The Jamestown S'Klallam tribe is hoping to develop something similar in Sequim. On the northwest tip of the Olympic Peninsula, the Makah tribe plans to build a motel. And the Quileute Tribe on the coast at La Push plans to build a hotel.

This kind of construction and development is based on the need to accommodate tourists. Visitors are interested in spending time on the reservations, and at present, few tribes can offer overnight accommodations.

Minorities Come to Washington

Just before statehood, about 3 percent of the people in Washington were Chinese. Throughout the country at that time, Chinese Americans were becoming the objects of suspicion and racism. This was especially true in areas such as Seattle and Tacoma, where labor unions were trying to expand. Union leaders thought that by targeting the Chinese, they could get white laborers to band together. In several towns, the Chinese were physically attacked and even killed. Nothing was done about the violence, however, because it was often backed by mayors and other political leaders. In Tacoma, the Chinese were forced to buy their own railway tickets out of town, while white agitators burned down their houses and businesses.

It was many decades before Chinese people began to move back into Washington. Other Asians, such as Vietnamese and Koreans, joined them. In the state's 1998 population count, Asians made up 4.84 percent of the people. Most of them live in the Seattle area.

Chinese Americans waiting for a performance of a Cantonese opera in Seattle

Prominent Asian Americans associated with Washington in recent years include Governor Gary Locke and Seattle native Minoru Yamasaki, the gifted architect of the World Trade Center in New York City and the spectacular Pacific Science Center in Seattle.

Hispanic people make up 6 percent of Washington's population. Many of them belong to families that have long been fruit pickers in eastern Washington. Many of the younger people in large eastern Washington communities are Hispanic, and this section of the population is growing more rapidly than others. Although the Yakima/Tri-Cities area has only 7 percent of the state's population, one-third of all the Hispanics in Washington live there.

Records indicate that a black servant named York traveled with the Lewis and Clark Expedition. He would have been the first African-American in the Washington area. Today, about 3.21 percent of the population is black.

Population of Washington's Major Cities (1990)

Seattle	516,259
Spokane	177,196
Tacoma	176,664
Bellevue	86,874
Everett	69,961
Federal Way	67,554

Public Education

Education in Washington began very early. A Native American of the Spokane tribe in the east opened a school for his people in 1833. He himself had been educated by a missionary. Marcus and Narcissa Whitman opened an Indian school at their Waiilatpu mission in 1837. Narcissa had been a teacher in Connecticut before marrying Marcus. When the Whitmans were killed in 1847, other Indian schools were closed out of fear.

In 1854, the Washington territorial legislature passed a law providing public schooling for all children starting at age four. However, the population was too scattered and there was never sufficient funds to build proper schools and hire enough teachers. Seven years later, an attempt to improve things were made by creating the post of territorial superintendent of education, but no real effort was made until statehood was achieved, when several high schools were opened.

The first time the U.S. government paid an existing school for the education of Indians was in 1869, to the Catholic school in Tulalip. In 1895, John Rankin Rogers, who would later be governor of the state, encouraged the "barefoot schoolboy law." This began the statewide public school system and guaranteed a certain amount of funding for each child, no matter how "barefoot." Children are not required to be in school until they are eight years old, but most start first grade at age seven.

Higher Education

A missionary built Whitman Seminary in Walla Walla in 1859 as a memorial to Dr. Marcus Whitman. It was the first college char-

Schoolchildren at a library in Newport, Washington

tered or approved by the territorial legislature. However, it closed down several times before it was chartered as Whitman College in 1883. It is still a high-quality small college.

The University of Washington opened in 1861 in Seattle as a territorial university. It had one building, one teacher—and one student! It was two decades before the legislature regularly funded the school and it could grow. In 1909, the university took over the buildings constructed for the Alaska-Yukon-Pacific Exposition. Today, it has about 35,000 students.

The University of Washington campus in Seattle

When Washington became a state, the new Washington legislature established an agricultural college—Washington State in Pullman—and two teacher's training colleges (called state normal schools)—Eastern Washington in Cheney and Central Washington in Ellensburg. Three years later, it added Western Washington in Bellingham. Today, they are all universities. WSU has more than 20,000 students; Eastern and Central have about 8,000 each; and Western has close to 12,000.

Gonzaga University at Spokane is a private, Catholic university founded in 1887. One of its most famous graduates was singer/actor Bing Crosby, who was born Harry Lillis Crosby in Tacoma and lived in Roslyn as a boy. He remained fond of Gonzaga and often referred to it in the movies he made with Bob Hope and on his television shows. The university today has a Crosby Library. In 2000, the school was a powerhouse in basketball.

CHAPTER TEN

Creative Fun

Washington offers the best of healthy, creative living, and many communities help keep it that way. For example, some Puget Sound communities have been redesigned for bicyclists. The Seattle-to-Portland Bicycle Classic is an annual 180-mile (290-km) bike ride.

Biking is one of the many outdoor sports that Washington residents enjoy.

For walkers, bikers, climbers, and skiers, Mount Rainier is a popular destination all year round. Climbing the spectacular mountain in summer is a challenge. In winter, the mountain offers climbing and skiing. Glaciers thousands of feet long entice many skiers. This kind of skiing can be very dangerous, though.

The Cascade Mountains have a longer ski season than anywhere else in the lower forty-eight states. Even in mid-July, people can ski on Mount Baker and other places in the Cascades. However, avalanches are increasingly frequent on these mountains. Mount Spokane and the Wenatchee Mountains have a shorter ski season.

Special kinds of snow adventures are available, too. Snowboarders enjoy Mount Baker. Night skiing is especially popular at Snoqualmie Pass. Helicopter skiing is also popular. Helicopters fly people to the untouched powder high in the mountains to ski in areas they couldn't reach by themselves.

Sun Mountain area in the Methow River valley in the northern Cascades has the second-largest network of cross-country ski trails

Opposite: Hiking in Mount Rainier National Park

Cross-country skiing in the Cascade Mountains

Climbing Mount Rainier

In 1870, Hazard Stevens, son of Territorial Governor Isaac I. Stevens, and his friend, Philemon Van Trump, may have become the first people to climb to the top of Mount Rainier. Twenty years later, Fay Fuller, a schoolteacher from Yelm, became the first woman to climb the mountain. It typically takes two days and one night to climb to the top and return. ■

in the United States. Hurricane Ridge in Olympic National Park is also a great place to cross-country ski.

Summer doesn't mean the end of trips to the mountains in Washington. Some chairlifts run in summer to transport picnickers and hikers to the top of mountains, including Crystal Mountain and White Pass near Mount Rainier.

The Water World

Puget Sound probably has more pleasure boats per person than anywhere else in the United States. Fishing for salmon and trout is especially good on the Columbia River and its tributaries.

Kayaking is very popular in Puget Sound. These flat, double-paddle boats are a great way to explore the area's many inlets and canals. Many kayakers take the Cascadia Marine Trail through the Olympic and San Juan Islands. More adventurous kayakers paddle white-water rivers with freezing water from melting glaciers in the mountains.

At Edmonds, just north of Seattle, a 300-foot (92-m)-long dry dock was sunk in the water in 1935. Along with other items deliberately placed in the water, it has become a scuba diver's delight. The fish like it, too.

Seattle's Lake Union is known for its Wooden Boat Center. Not only are the wooden boats of old cherished and displayed, but they float and can be rowed by devotees. Each July, the Wooden Boat Festival is held here.

A marina on Puget Sound

Team Sports

The oldest professional sports team in Washington is the Super-Sonics. This Seattle basketball team began playing in 1967. They have won the National Basketball Association championship only once—in 1979. The SuperSonics play at KeyArena (yes, it's one word). The Seattle Thunderbirds play ice hockey here.

A group of Seattle businessmen, headed by Lloyd W. Nordstrom, worked to get a National Football League franchise for the city and built the first Kingdome stadium in 1972. This is where the Seahawks play.

The name *Seahawks* was selected from 20,365 entries and 1,741 different names. On August 1, 1976, the Seahawks played their first game, against San Francisco, in front of 60,825 fans in the Kingdome.

The Seattle SuperSonics play in Key Arena.

Seattle Pilots

Seattle's first Major League Baseball team existed for one season—1969–1970. The Seattle Pilots were an expansion team in the American League. Although the team won its first game against the California Angels, it did not attract fan support. After only one season, the team disbanded. ■

The next year, the Seahawks hosted the Pro Bowl. The team has won only one division championship, in 1988. They have never made it to the Super Bowl.

The Kingdome is now being replaced. Voters approved a new stadium for the Seahawks, owned by billionaire Paul Allen, in 1997. It was imploded in March 2000. The new stadium will seat 45,658 fans in luxury seating and boxes.

Washington's Major League Baseball team is the Seattle Mariners. They played their first game on April 6, 1977, at the Kingdome. The new home of the Seattle Mariners, Safeco Field, opened in 1999.

Other professional teams in Washington include the Seattle Fire of the Women's National Basketball Association and the Seattle Sounders soccer team.

Other areas of Washington concentrate on minor league baseball. Its minor league teams include the Spokane Indians, affiliated with the Kansas City Royals; the Yakima Bears, affiliated with the Los Angeles Dodgers; and the Tacoma Rainiers and the Everett Aquasox, both affiliated with the Seattle Mariners.

Safeco Field is home to the Seattle Mariners.

Since 1981, the University of Washington Huskies, who play in the Pacific-10, have played in the Rose Bowl seven times and won their fourth Rose Bowl game in 2001. The Washington State Cougars are also in the Pacific-10, but they haven't been lucky enough to play in the Rose Bowl since 1931.

Seattle Slew

One of the few racehorses to win the Triple Crown was a thoroughbred named Seattle Slew. He captured the Kentucky Derby, the Belmont Stakes, and the Preakness in one year.

But Seattle Slew wasn't from Seattle. The owners lived in White Swan, on the eastern side of the Cascades.

In 1977, the horse stunned everyone by winning the Triple Crown. Since then he has been in demand for breeding. ■

Art in Washington

The state's art is a wonderful mix of styles. Native American totem poles, now recognized as art, are found throughout the state, especially in Seattle. The Indians of the Northwest used a tree called canoe cedar to carve their totem poles and to make single-log dugout canoes.

The Seattle Art Museum displays items from around the world, as well as a major collection of Northwest Coast Native American

The hammering man outside the Seattle Art Museum

Ray Charles played in many Seattle clubs during the 1940s.

art. At the front of the museum, a 48-foot (15-m)-tall flat, steel sculpture of a worker moves a hammer up and down, day in and day out. In 1994, when the Seattle Art Museum moved to new quarters, its old building in Volunteer Park became the Seattle Asian Art Museum.

The city of Seattle budgets money for art every year. The result is impressive "sidewalk art." Statues and murals show up in unexpected places, making walking through the city a joy.

Rocking Seattle

Georgia-born jazz and blues great Ray Charles, who became blind as a child, got his start in Seattle. He worked the clubs there in the 1940s. It was in Seattle that he met the younger composer/singer Quincy Jones. The two have won numerous Grammy Awards over the years and played an important role in the development of rock and roll music.

Seattle rock singer and guitarist Jimi Hendrix formed a group called the Jimi Hendrix Experience in 1966. He became an instant success with his first album the next year. Hendrix, born in 1942 in Seattle, was part African-American and part Native American. Although he could not read music, he experimented with electronic music to create completely new sounds. Hendrix changed forever how the electric guitar was played. He died in 1970 of a drug overdose.

Seattle's rock music did not end with Hendrix. Kurt Cobain, born in Hoquiam in 1967, formed an alternative hard-rock group called Nirvana. It became *the* group of the early 1990s. Nirvana's musical success brought Seattle lots of attention. The group's gui-

Guitarist Jimi Hendrix was born in Seattle.

tar style was given the tongue-in-cheek name of "grunge." Grunge became the name for that kind of alternative music as well as the band's dressing style of baggy clothing, torn jeans, and combat boots.

In 1995, the year Nirvana won a Grammy Award, a Seattle group called Pearl Jam won a Grammy for best hard rock performance. Seattle guitarist Stone Gossard had put together the band with Eddie Vedder, Mike McCready, Jeff Ament, and David Abbruzzese. They named their group Pearl Jam after Vedder's great-grandmother Pearl, who was famous for her jam. They issued their first album, *Ten,* ten days after the group got together.

More Traditional Music

Like so many other cultural institutions, the Seattle Symphony Orchestra, founded in 1903, has benefited from the growth of Seattle. In 1998, it moved into the new Benaroya Performance Hall, which has a large concert hall and a smaller, more intimate recital hall. The older Seattle Center still houses the Seattle Opera.

Construction of the Experience Music Project

Paul Allen, one of the founders of Microsoft, has created a completely interactive, musical museum called the Experience Music Project (EMP) in Seattle, which opened in 2000. It features exhibits about Jimi Hendrix, the history of rock and roll, the development of the electric guitar, and much more. World-famous architect Frank Gehry designed the building. EMP also organizes children's music camps.

Many music festivals are held throughout the state, especially in summer. In August, the city of Bellingham puts on a music festival and the Chalk Art Festival. Everyone from children to professional artists take up colored chalks to decorate the city's sidewalks, with the hope that it won't rain!

The internationally known Joffrey Ballet company started in Seattle. Robert Joffrey was born and trained in Seattle. His ballet company is now headquartered in Chicago, Illinois.

Writers and Artists

Many artists and writers have found Washington a great place to be creative. African-American artist Jacob Lawrence, who lived in Seattle, has been called a storyteller of the black American experience. Aberdeen-born artist Robert Motherwell was known for his abstract expressionist paintings.

Writers from Washington include novelists Ernest K. Gann, Don Berry, and Ivan Doig. Novelist Frank Herbert, creator of the science-fiction world of *Dune,* was a native of Tacoma and lived in Port Townsend on the Olympic Peninsula.

Theodore Roethke was a famous Washington poet. He moved to Washington after World War II and quickly earned the title the Poet of Puget Sound. His poetry was a lyrical tribute to the beauty and restlessness of nature in the Northwest. Following in his footsteps was Carolyn Kizer, a native of Spokane and founder of *Poetry Northwest* magazine.

The Far Side is the weird cartoon world of Washington cartoonist Gary Larson. Writer Susan McCarthy described Larson's world as "entirely populated by the lumpy, the big-nosed, the bespectacled, the bug-eyed, and the foofy-haired." Born in Tacoma in 1950, Larson is known for his irreverent humor. His first cartoons were published in the *Seattle Times*, which fired him because they offended too many readers. Since then, Gary Larson's fans have been too busy laughing to be offended.

Theodore Roethke was known as the Poet of Puget Sound.

Timeline

United States History

1607 The first permanent English settlement is established in North America at Jamestown.

1620 Pilgrims found Plymouth Colony, the second permanent English settlement.

1776 America declares its independence from Britain.

1783 The Treaty of Paris officially ends the Revolutionary War in America.

1787 The U.S. Constitution is written.

1803 The Louisiana Purchase almost doubles the size of the United States.

1812–15 The United States and Britain fight the War of 1812.

1861–65 The North and South fight each other in the American Civil War.

Washington State History

1790 Spanish explorers build the first European fort in Washington at Neah Bay on the northern tip of the Olympic Peninsula.

1805 Lewis and Clark reach the mouth of the Columbia River on November 15.

1811 The Canadian Northwest Fur Company establishes a fur-trading post at Spokane.

1832 Nathaniel Wyeth and William Sublette pioneer the Oregon Trail from the Missouri River to the Columbia River.

1833 A member of the Spokane tribe opens one of the first schools in Washington.

1848 The U.S. government creates Oregon Territory, which included present-day Washington.

1854 Washington Territory holds its first election on January 30.

1855 Chief Sealth, a Salish Indian, signs a treaty giving the land around Puget Sound to the United States.

United States History

The United States is **1917–18**
involved in World War I.

The stock market crashes, **1929**
plunging the United States into
the Great Depression.

The United States **1941–45**
fights in World War II.
The United States becomes a **1945**
charter member of the U.N.

The United States **1951–53**
fights in the Korean War.

The U.S. Congress enacts a series of **1964**
groundbreaking civil rights laws.

The United States **1964–73**
engages in the Vietnam War.

The United States and other **1991**
nations fight the brief
Persian Gulf War against Iraq.

Washington State History

1883 The Northern Pacific Railroad links
Washington with the East.

1889 The U.S. Congress admits Washington
to the Union as the forty-second state
on November 11. Fifty-eight blocks of
Seattle burn in the Great Seattle Fire.

1903 The Seattle Symphony Orchestra is
founded.

1916 William E. Boeing founds the world's
largest airplane company.

1938 Olympic National Park is created as
part of President Franklin Roosevelt's
New Deal.

1942 President Roosevelt orders thousands
of people of Japanese descent
removed from Washington to intern-
ment camps until World War II is
ended.

1962 Seattle's world's fair is held.

1980 Mount St. Helens erupts, killing fifty-
seven people and destroying hundreds
of thousands of acres of forestland.

1996 Gary Locke is elected the nation's first
Chinese-American governor.

Fast Facts

Statehood date November 11, 1889, the 42nd state

Origin of state name Named for the first president of the United States, George Washington

State capital Olympia

State nickname The Evergreen State

State motto *Al-ki* (an Indian word meaning "Bye and Bye")

State flower Coast, or western, rhododendron

State bird Willow goldfinch or wild canary

State tree Western hemlock

State fish Steelhead trout

State fruit Apple

State grass Bluebunch wheatgrass

State insect Green darner dragonfly

State fossil Columbian mammoth

State gem Petrified wood

State dance Square dance

State ship *President Washington*

State tartan Washington state tartan

State capitol

The Evergreen State

Washingtonians

State song	"Washington, My Home"
State fairs	Western Washington in Puyallup (September); Central Washington in Yakima (late September); Evergreen State Fair in Monroe (late August)
Total area; rank	70,637 sq. mi. (182,950 sq km); 19th
Land; rank	66,581 sq. mi. (172,445 sq km); 20th
Water; rank	4,056 sq. mi. (10,505 sq km); 9th
Inland water; rank	1,545 sq. mi. (4,002 sq km); 14th
Coastal water; rank	2,511 sq. mi. (6,503 sq km); 2nd
Geographic center	Chelan, 10 miles (16 km) southwest of Wenatchee
Latitude and longitude	Washington is located approximately between 49° and 45° 30′ N and 117° and 124° 45′ W
Highest point	Mount Rainier, 14,410 feet (4,395 m)
Lowest point	Sea level along the coast
Largest city	Seattle
Number of counties	39
Population; rank	4,887,941 (1990 census); 18th
Density	72 persons per sq. mi. (28 per sq km)
Population distribution	76% urban, 24% rural

Ethnic distribution (does not equal 100%)

White	90.14%
Hispanic	6.00%
Asian and Pacific Islanders	4.84%
African-American	3.21%
Native American	1.81%

Mount Rainier National Park

Record high temperature	118°F (48°C) in Grant County on July 24, 1928, and at Ice Harbor Dam on August 5, 1961
Record low temperature	–48°F (–44°C) at Mazama and Winthrop on December 30, 1968
Average July temperature	66°F (19°C)
Average January temperature	30°F (–1°C)
Average annual precipitation	38 inches (97 cm)

National Parks

Mount Rainier National Park includes Mount Rainier, an ancient volcano, and dense forests and meadows.

North Cascades National Park is a rugged mountain area with glaciers and dramatic waterfalls.

Olympic National Park has 922,651 acres (373,674 ha) of mountain wilderness, lakes, massive trees, and temperate rain forests.

National Historical Parks, Reserves, and Sites

Ebey's Landing National Historical Reserve preserves the Puget Sound exploration and settlement.

Fort Vancouver National Historic Site preserves the western headquarters of Hudson's Bay Company's fur-trading facilities.

Klondike Gold Rush National Historical Park honors the state's starting point for prospectors heading to the Yukon goldfields in 1896.

Nez Perce National Historical Park commemorates the culture and traditions of the Nez Perce people.

San Juan Island National Historical Park marks the peaceful resolution of a boundary dispute between British and American troops.

Whitman Mission National Historic Site preserves the mission of Marcus and Narcissa Whitman.

Hiking in Mount Rainier National Park

National Recreation Areas

Lake Chelan National Recreation Area contains the Stehekin Valley and adjoins North Cascades National Park.

Lake Roosevelt National Recreation Area preserves the lake formed by the Grand Coulee Dam.

Ross Lake National Recreation Area preserves parts of the Skagit River.

National Forests

Washington has eight national forests.

Sports Teams

NCAA Teams (Division 1)

Eastern Washington University Eagles

Gonzaga University Bulldogs/Zags (basketball only)

University of Washington Huskies

Washington State University Cougars

Major League Baseball

Seattle Mariners

National Basketball Association

Seattle SuperSonics

National Football League

Seattle Seahawks

Cultural Institutions

Libraries

Washington State Library (Olympia) is the state's oldest library.

The Seattle Public Library contains fine collections on the Pacific Northwest and on aeronautics.

The University of Washington Library (Seattle) contains major collections on East Asia, Pacific Northwest history, and the fishing industry.

Safeco Field

The University of
Washington

Museums

The Thomas Burke Memorial Washington State Museum (Seattle)
features exhibits on natural history and Native Americans.

Seattle Art Museum has fine collections of African and Northwest
Native American art.

Performing Arts

Washington has one major opera company, two major symphony
orchestras, and one major dance company.

Universities and Colleges

In the late 1990s, Washington had 37 public and 27 private
institutions of higher learning.

Annual Events

January–March

International Boat Show in Seattle (January)

Northwest Bach Festival in Spokane (January)

Great Bavarian Ice Fest in Leavenworth (January)

International Snowshoe Softball Tournament in Winthrop (January)

Tacoma Dome Boat Show in Tacoma (February)

Upper Skagit Bald Eagle Festival (February)

Annual Gray Whale Migration in Westport and Ocean Shores
  (March)

April–June

Cherry Blossom and Japanese Cultural Festival in Seattle (April)

Apple Blossom Festival in Wenatchee (late April and early May)

Yachting and boating season opening in Puget Sound (May 1)

Lilac Festival and Bloomsday Footrace in Spokane (May)

Rhododendron Festival in Port Townsend (late May)

June Blues Festival and Workshop in Port Townsend (June)

The Washington State
International Kite
Festival

July–September

Toppenish Indian Pow Wow in Toppenish (July 3–4)

Pacific Northwest Arts and Crafts Fair in Bellevue (July)

King County Fair in Enumclaw (July)

Seafair in Seattle (July and August)

International Kite Festival on the Long Beach Peninsula (August)

Ellensburg Rodeo (early September)

Western Washington State Fair in Puyallup (September)

Autumn Leaf Festival in Leavenworth (late September and early October)

October–December

Yule Log Festival in Poulsbo (December)

Ray Charles

Famous People

Kurt Cobain (1967–1994)	Musician
Bing Crosby (1904–1977)	Singer and actor
William O. Douglas (1898–1980)	Supreme Court justice
William Henry (Bill) Gates (1955–)	Software programmer and entrepreneur
Jimi Hendrix (1942–1970)	Musician
Chief Joseph (1840?–1904)	Indian leader
Mary McCarthy (1912–1989)	Writer
Edward R. Murrow (1908–1965)	News broadcaster
Chief Sealth (1786?–1866)	Indian leader

Jimi Hendrix

To Find Out More

History

- Doherty, Craig A., and Katherine M. Doherty. *The Seattle Space Needle*. Woodbridge, Conn.: Blackbirch, 1997.

- Fradin, Dennis Brindell. *Washington*. Chicago: Childrens Press, 1994.

- Nelson, Sharlene P. *Mount St. Helens National Volcanic Monument*. Danbury, Conn.: Children's Press, 1997.

- Stein, Conrad. *Seattle*. Danbury, Conn.: Children's Press, 1999.

- Thompson, Kathleen. *Washington*. Austin, Tex.: Raintree/Steck Vaughn, 1996.

Biography

- Montgomery, Elizabeth Rider, and Russ Hoover (illustrator). *Chief Seattle: Great Statesman*. Champaign, Ill.: Garrard Publishing Co., 1966.

- Raatma, Lucia. *Bill Gates: Software Programmer and Entrepreneur*. Chicago: Ferguson Publishing, 2000.

Fiction

- Hamm, Diane Johnston, and Paul Micic (illustrator). *Daughter of Suqua*. Chicago: Albert Whitman, 1997.

- Holm, Jennifer L. *Our Only May Amelia*. New York: Harper Collins, 1999.

- Sharpe, Susan. *Spirit Quest*. New York: Puffin, 1993.

Websites

- **State of Washington**
  http://www.state.wa.us/
  The official state website

- **Washington State Historical Society**
  http://www.wshs.org/
  For online exhibit tours and more

Addresses

- **Department of Community, Trade, and Economic Development**
  Tourism Development Division
  P.O. Box 42500
  Olympia, WA 98504
  For information about travel and tourism in Washington

- **Department of Community, Trade, and Economic Development**
  Market and Targeted Industry Development
  2001 Sixth Avenue
  Suite 2600
  Seattle, WA 98121
  For information about Washington's industry

- **Superintendent of Public Instruction**
  Old Capitol Building
  P.O. Box 47200
  Olympia, WA 98504-7200
  For information about Washington's government and history

Index

Page numbers in *italics* indicate illustrations.

Meet the Author

Jean F. Blashfield's first trip to Washington was for a meeting with the fantasy company Wizards of the Coast. She found Washington to be a fantasy of its own. She looks forward to returning to investigate the many different sides of the state.

During her many years working in publishing, Jean F. Blashfield lived in Chicago; London, England; and Washington, D.C. When she married Wallace Black (a Chicago publisher, writer, and pilot), they moved northward to Wisconsin. Today, she has two college-age children, three cats, and two computers in her Victorian home in Delavan, Wisconsin.

Jean F. Blashfield has written close to one hundred books, most of them for young people. She likes best to write about interesting places, but she loves history and science, too. She has created an encyclopedia of aviation and space, written popular books

on murderers and house plants, and had a lot of fun creating an early book on the things women have done, called *Hellraisers, Heroines, and Holy Women*.

In Wisconsin, she delighted in finding TSR, Inc., the publishers of the *Dungeons & Dragons* games. At that company, she founded a new department to publish fantasy gamebooks and novels, and helped the company expand into a worldwide enterprise.

She and her husband later formed their own company, which took advantage of Jean's massive collection of 3 x 5 cards. The cards contained interesting tidbits of information about many states, their places, and their people. Today, she has all that research on computer. In fact, she uses computers to broaden her research on Washington and many other subjects. She also produces whole books on the computer—scanning pictures, creating layouts, and creating the index. She has become an avid Internet surfer and is working on her own website, but she'll never give up her trips to the library.

Photo Credits